Recognizing & Managing Aggression

Practical Awareness Startegies & Defensive Tactics

Jesse Lawn

Copyright Jesse Lawn 2011

Special Thanks to...

My Wife, Laura, for all of her technical help with the production of this book

Richard Dimitri, for all of the support and friendship over the years

Table of Contents

Introduction	4
Operational Security Model	6
Active Scanning	9
Threat Recognition	12
Personal Perimeter	38
Diffusion and De-escalation	43
Defensive Countermeasures	63
Tactical Disengagement	83
Aid and Evacuation	90
Post-Conflict Police Interaction	101
Conclusion	103
Sources	105

Introduction

What is violence? Violence is generally defined as physical force exerted for the purpose of violating, damaging, or abusing. In reality, violence is a tool. It's not good or bad. It's what we do with it that matters. A police officer who shoots a homicidal maniac on a shooting spree is using violence as a tool for good. A rapist is using violence for evil.

Like it or not, violence is a part of the human experience. Not only is violence used in the commission of crimes, but it determines the boundaries by which we live and is used to enforce the laws of the land. In our society, violence is extremely prevalent…even glorified. Our cinematic heroes are often violent killers. Our video games are graphic simulations of horrific experiences. In general, our social conditioning encourages violence as a means to an end and a way to gain status. Consider the Navy SEALS, for example. Everyone worships those guys. They kill people, lots of people…and they're absolutely our society's heroes.

Before you decide on a personal protection regimen, you first need to make some ethical decisions. Can you use violence? How far are you capable of going to defend yourself? Can you kill another person? Could you gouge out an eye? Some can't. Some religious people are forbidden from such acts, even in self defense. Some physicians and medical professionals refuse to on moral ground. You need to be clear on what you are okay with. For example, if you don't think you can kill someone who's trying to hurt you…don't get a concealed carry license and buy a gun. On the same note, if you don't think you'd have a moral or ethical problem blasting a hole in someone who was trying to kill you…by all means, get a gun. The key here is to evaluate this stuff ahead of time. You don't want to be in a life or death situation, pull out a gun and freeze…only to realize that you can't pull the trigger.

Operational Security Model

Complete personal protection encompasses more than the mere application of physical fighting techniques or the use of a weapon. In order to provide any true measure of safety, we must first step back and look at the bigger picture. Effectively evaluating the grander scheme of things requires specific training and a broader mindset. "Operational security" is a term that refers to the overall ability to perceive and manage threats to your safety. In order to ensure optimum efficiency, it's important to establish and follow a standard model.

Following an appropriate standard model gives you several advantages; it increases your environmental and situational awareness, reduces confusion in the chaos of the moment, demonstrates your commitment to avoiding conflict (which can be quite helpful in court), ensures you act in a just and appropriate manner, and promotes confidence. However, if something is going to be made a standard, it needs to meet certain criteria. An "Operational Security Model" (OSM) must be simple yet practical, versatile, comprehensive, ethical, and legal. The OSM I advocate is comprised of the following components:

- **Active scanning**

- **Threat recognition**

- **Personal perimeter management**

- **Diffusion and de-escalation**

- **Defensive countermeasures**

- **Tactical disengagement**

- **Aid and evacuation**

Here is a brief explanation of the theory behind the OSM; an active scan allows us to perceive potential threats before they are upon us. Once a threat has been identified, we can use a variety of techniques to create space between us and the danger. If the danger is a person, and they aggressively pursue us, often times it's possible to deter them from becoming violent by using verbal skills diffuse the situation. However, because not everyone is reasonable or interested in negotiation, we may need to physically defend ourselves. That's where the defensive countermeasures come in. Using whatever training and tools we have, we fend off a physical assault until it is safe to tactically disengage. Recognize that once the fight is over, the situation may not be completely in hand. If you or someone you are travelling with is wounded…you'll need to render aid and get them and/or yourself to safety.

As you can see, the components all fit together in a supporting cycle. That being said, there are times when steps of the OSM must be skipped or omitted. For example, there is no need to verbally diffuse a situation where someone in a car is trying to run you over. You will want to use all of the other steps…but notice how the OSM is not "hard-and-fast". It's flexible. Further, it facilitates defense of the three primary areas of personal sanctity: physical safety, psychological well being, and personal privacy. These are the three things a bodyguard is required to protect in a client. You are your own bodyguard.

All of my programs and outlines, including this manual, currently follow this OSM.

Active Scanning

Our defensive capabilities are directly related to our awareness. The function of the active scan is to proactively seek out and identify any potential threat. While hostilities and acts of violence certainly constitute serious threats, threats are not necessarily combative in nature. One must remember that environmental hazards such as vehicular traffic, sharp objects, electrical wires, and random obstacles account for more traumatic injuries than violent confrontations. An active scan should provide maximum environmental awareness.

Obviously, the world is a big place, and we cannot possibly scan every inch of our environment as we move about on a daily basis. There's simply too much visual stimuli to process effectively. A good general guideline to follow when conducting an active scan is to survey a 360 degree, 20 ft. "bubble" around you. Based on numerous studies, a 20 ft. "bubble" provides, on average, 1.5 seconds+ to perceive and react to an incoming threat. Seeing what is in front of you at that distance is relatively easy. Keeping a visual on the space behind you takes a little more effort.

To exercise effective 360 degree awareness, keep your head up and look slightly above the horizon in front of you. By looking upwards, your peripheral vision will be able to take a more dominant role in your active scan, enabling you to observe a larger area at one time. Looking up will also help you notice possible threats at or above your head level. Untrained individuals tend to have tunnel vision, looking only at what lies directly in front of them and specific areas of interest. Be sure to survey the entire scene around you by casually looking from side to side. When your head is turned to one side or the other, your peripheral vision will catch people and objects approaching you from the rear. This technique is referred to as the "head-on-a-swivel" by tactical professionals.

Another key component to an active scan is posture. By standing up straight, your head-on-a-swivel technique will be much more effective. Not only will your visual range be improved, but you will exhibit a confident, aware body language. This body language sends a clear message to any would-be attackers; you are likely to notice them and there's a good likelihood that you would resist…making for a difficult criminal encounter. Criminals like easy victims. They generally go by the adage, "if it looks like a duck, it's probably a duck". Look like a Hawk.

Your active scan should not only be seeking out potential threats, but also possible exits and evacuation routes in case you need to leave in a hurry. The best way to avoid injury and heartache is to not be in the danger zone when bad things happen. Whenever possible, try to navigate the locations with the most avenues of open passage in your immediate area. The main function of the active scan is to conduct constant reconnaissance of the ever changing environment within your 20 ft. bubble. Never turn it off.

Threat Recognition

As I mentioned earlier, there are lots of different types and classifications of threats. This manual, however, is about managing aggression. As such, I'm only going to address violent threats in this section. Violent threats are almost always the result of other people's negative intention. Considering that violence comes from negative people, threat recognition in this case is comprised of recognizing criminal behavior and pre-assault indicators.

Before we get into detail about the different behavioral dynamics, there are a few general assumptions I have for dealing with angry people. **Rule number one, "Everyone is armed".** Think about it. Just about every guy I know carries a pocket knife of some sort. Even in jails and prisons where weapons are forbidden, inmates still create things to stab each other with. Oh, by the way, those guys are released every day… When they get out, one of the first things they do is arm up. Most cons aren't comfortable without something to poke people with. Knives aren't the only common weapon. What about hand guns? Concealed carry licenses are regularly issued by just about every state in the union. That doesn't even begin to account for all of the illegal concealed carry happening. I assure you, there are far more people carrying concealed illegally, than legally. Hey, if it turns out that the angry person doesn't pull out a weapon and try and kill you…great. It's best to be prepared.

Rule number two, "Everyone has friends". You do. Guess what? Even if they're an asshole…they have friends too. Chances are, you are in their territory if they have decided to become aggressive with you. That means their friends are very likely to be nearby, or on their way…even if you don't see them. Never assume you are in a one-on-one fight. You may feel like you are, right up until someone starts stabbing you in the back.

Rule number three, "Nothing good comes out of pockets or waistlines during a conflict". Reference rule number one…"Everyone is armed". If someone rapidly stuffs their hand in their pants while they're yelling obscenities at you, chances are, that's not a business card coming out. Do yourself a favor, and get in the habit of watching people's hands. It's common to hear martial arts instructors say things like, "watch his eyes" or "watch the center of his chest". The reality is that they are going to hit you, grab you, or draw a weapon on you with their hands. Watch the hands.

Now that we have our basic assumptions covered, let's talk about behavioral dynamics. The stereotypical "evil bad guy" that Hollywood offers us is not the threat you are likely to face. That doesn't mean that an armed psycho wired on a meth cocktail won't attack you in a dark parking lot with the intent of dismembering you and wearing your skin as a new coat. We will, of course, prepare ourselves for the potential of dealing with a true predator, but most conflict occurs within the boundaries of social violence.

Social Violence

What is social violence? Social violence is violence based on natural human vs. human conflict. Unpleasant as it may be, human beings don't always get along, and they don't always solve their problems peacefully. In a perfect world, we would move beyond this, but somehow…we never seem to make it. Social violence usually escalates from challenges or disputes over territory, status, or perceived violations of social rule.

The goal of an aggressor in a social setting is usually to establish a position of physical and psychological dominance in order to become or remain the Alpha. Rarely does this involve maiming or killing.

That's not to say that a serious injury, or even a mortal wound cannot be sustained in an outburst of social violence, but that is not typically the outcome. What does this mean for us? It means not all bad guys are created equal. From a legal perspective, when it comes to social violence, lethal force as a self defense option is almost certainly off of the table.

Fortunately, social violence is relatively easy to spot. It follows a very predictable pattern, which we see repeated throughout the animal kingdom, and it is almost always preceded by verbal communication. Let's talk about ritual male posturing. Guys do this in every species. They puff up and try to intimidate the other male into backing down or behaving in a submissive manner. Human males tend to draw their shoulders back and stick out their chests, make fierce eye contact, and make an obvious attempt to invade the other man's personal space. This ritualized behavior is a clear indicator that you have a potentially violent person on your hands. If you recognize that this behavior happening in your presence, leave.

Social Violence Pattern:

- *Eye contact*
- *Ritual posturing*
- *Invasion of personal space*
- *Touching/pushing*
- *Haymaker/tackle*

Aggressive males often have a very active scan, much like I advocate for security purposes. The big difference is theirs is designed to be invasive and intimidating. Angry people see everyone as the enemy. They look for other people to challenge for alpha status and also for those who exhibit signs of weakness and smell like prey. Many social conflicts begin with "mad-dogging", the street term for a fierce gaze.

Once the aggressor takes notice of the potential victim, he will immediately attempt to appear intimidating and dangerous. Here we see the shoulders come back and the chest come out. Sometimes this action is accompanied by a bouncy gait. This is akin to a peacock strut. It's a show, pure and simple. Most of the time, I doubt they consciously realize they're doing it. Such predictable involuntary movement does not provide a tactical advantage, especially when it places their vulnerable anatomy in compromising positions.

Before any physical attack is launched, the aggressor will almost always have some "jawing" to do. In order to be as intimidating as possible, the verbal thrashing or threatening is usually delivered at an uncomfortably close range. Often, an aggressor will get right in your face…nose to nose. An invasion of personal space makes a huge statement and has a profound psychological impact. Consider the reasons behind social violence. This person is probably jockeying for status, trying to get you to acknowledge their territorial claim, or "teach you a lesson" of some sort. If there is no verbal communication, they cannot measure their progress or get verification of their victory. At this stage, many situations can be verbally de-escalated and diffused before things turn violent, especially if you have the right training.

If they have no interest in negotiation, their next step will likely be to measure your resolve by poking or pushing at you. Actions like slapping a hat off your head or knocking something out of your hand also fall into this category. Essentially, they are working themselves up to a higher level of violence while checking to see whether or not you offer significant resistance. The good news is they feel the need to work themselves up to violence. Remember that Hollywood style predator we were talking about earlier? That's not this guy. However, once they are comfortable and ready, they will most commonly launch a "haymaker at your grill", though, football style tackles are almost as common. While this is not a good thing, at least this kind of attack is relatively easy to predict and defend against.

There are often many pre-assault indicators to the actual physical attack:

Body posture-

The tense, rigid posture of an angry person is easy to spot. The back is typically straight, while the head and neck extend forward. As mentioned before, the shoulders back and the chest puffed out in a ritualized presentation are also quite common.

Sudden change in eye contact –

Beware of an angry glaring stare that suddenly breaks away from you for no apparent reason. Often this is a psychological distraction to catch you off guard. The distraction could be designed to set you up for the attack that incapacitates you. Likewise, be mindful of someone who goes from a disinterested look to an intense glare. The sudden change in eye communication is significant.

Facial expressions –

While this one may seem obvious, in the heat of the moment, you'd be surprised at the things people miss. Sometimes, a person may say something verbally, but their facial expression says something entirely different…giving them away. For example, someone may say that something tasted good, but if they didn't like it, their face tells the truth. The face lies less than words.

Color change –

A sudden change in pallor is never a good thing. If someone is so upset that they hold their breath or work enough blood up into their head to turn their face red and cause their facial veins to pulse…they're pretty mad. That much anger can push people to do crazy things on the spur of the moment. Also, if a person suddenly goes white or pale, that's very bad. It means they are about to get physical. All of the blood in their face and core is moving to their limbs to fight. It's a sign of the adrenal response.

"Woofing"-

"Woofing" is a term made popular in the industry by FAST instructor, Bill Kipp. It's basically just them barking at you. The more intense the verbiage, the more likely the attack. Often, an aggressor needs to work himself up to the physical element of his assault. Woofing can be used to intimidate, but also to as a form of self-encouragement for the aggressor. They may even tell you what they are about to do, like a bad movie monologue.

"Crack" in voice -

When people are heavily adrenalized, their speech patterns are often affected. A common side effect of an adrenal stress spike is the faltering of the voice. If their voice cracks, squeaks, goes into a higher pitch, or anything of the like, consider it a warning sign. They are likely about to act.

Invasion of personal space –

This one we should recognize as one of the elements of the social violence pattern, in fact, the one that directly precedes physical contact. If someone invades your personal space, they do not mean you well. Someone who will violate your space probably doesn't have any compunction about invading it a little further in the form of an assault. They may be testing the waters or they may be setting you up. One way or the other, now you know they can hurt you. They are "within range".

Balled fists –

If someone flexes their fingers into fists, that's a tell-tale sign that they want to hit you. Someone who wants to hit you isn't far from deciding to hit you.

Clenched jaw –

When the body is adrenalized, it tends to tense up. As this happens, the muscles in the jaw follow suit. Rolling, flexing mandibular muscles are an obvious indicator of anger. The teeth may clamp together and perhaps grind. This causes any speech to be spoken through the teeth. This level of tension is an advanced symptom of adrenal stress. Someone this far along is likely close to snapping.

Rocking back and forth –

A person whose body begins rocking back and forth is either so adrenalized that they cannot hold still, or developing a comfortable rhythm to launch an attack. Neither of these is good for you. As we've already discussed, someone in a highly adrenalized state is very dangerous, as is someone gaining psychological momentum to attack.

Agitated twitch –

Twitches can develop when people are under extreme stress. Facial twitches of the lips, nose, and eyes are very common. Think of an animal snarling right before it attacks. Also, leg and arm twitches signify the intent to move suddenly. Law enforcement officers all know the twitchy leg that says, "I'm going to run any second".

Violent arm waving –

Violent movement is an indicator of impending violent action. When the arms start flailing about, the probability of them being directed at you is high. Also, moving limbs are difficult to visually track and can be quite distracting. If an aggressor exhibits this unpredictable behavior, consider it a significant threat.

Chimp "arm-pump" –

Similar to violent arm waving, the "chimp pump", as I like to call it, occurs when an aggressive person's arms bow out at the elbows and their fists pump up and down like coordinated pistons. Often this ridiculous looking action is accompanied by hopping and dancing about. I call this the "chimp pump" because chimpanzees perform the exact same behavior when they are excited or agitated. It's a very energetic behavior that is indicative of working themselves up to a physical attack.

Aggressive touching –

Any invasive physical contact counts. Examples of aggressive touching include facial contact, pushing, poking, slapping, flicking, disturbing clothing, or batting at objects in your possession. During moments of peak aggression, it is most common for an aggressor to touch for your face. Likewise, they may press their face into you. The face is the physical/visual representation of the individual. If they are at all mad at you, this is the area people tend to focus on, psychologically speaking.

Now that we are clear on the pattern of social violence and some fundamental pre-assault indicators, let's back up for just a moment. A few paragraphs up, I mentioned some common reasons behind social violence. Author Rory Miller, has very aptly named these three common behavioral motivations:

The "Status Seeking Show"

The "Educational Beatdown"

The "Territorial Display"

The "Status Seeking Show" is all about making progress on the perceived hierarchy. In order to gain social standing, in whatever arena they are concerned with, they intend to appear intimidating and dominant. Depending on the situation, a status seeking show could be all bark or it can be deadly. A young punk trying to prove he's tough to gain face in front of some buddies is one side of the spectrum, whereas the other is the inner-city hommie who's trying to gain a reputation in his neighborhood for being the "hardest" gangbanger in the hood. The youngster will probably bark a lot, while the gangster will use violence AS the show. One way or the other, it's an exhibition of their aggressive intent and a declaration of alpha status.

An "Educational Beatdown" is a form of social discipline, vigilante style. When a self-appointed "Alpha" perceives what they believe to be a "violation" of a social or personal directive…they may feel the need to impose a physical beating as both a message and a form of punishment. The beating is designed to "teach" the offender a lesson and reinforce that the aggressor holds more status on the hierarchy. While the educational beatdown is by no means limited to street gangs, this method is a standard operating procedure for most criminal gangs. This is how they establish rank and file in their own organization. The educational beatdown can also be administered by the jackass at the bar that believes that only guys in cowboy hats are allowed to dance with pretty women. Further, incidents of domestic violence where a spouse is beaten into submission also illustrate this concept. The specific infraction is not as important as the offender's need to "show you".

A "Territorial Display" is an attempt to display ownership or special claim over a specific person or place. People can become territorial over just about anything. Territorial displays occur over potential mates, private property and border disputes, frequented locations/ establishments, cars, tools, equipment, etc. The goal is often, not only to defend the territory and expel an intruder…but also to demonstrate courage and resolve. This makes for a dangerous situation. An aggressive person who feels their dominance is challenged in a place they consider their home "turf" is very likely to become violent. This is actually a common behavior in all mammals.

Now, each of the above motivations is bad enough when demonstrated by a single individual, but what about when more than one person is involved? Anytime you have a group turning on a perceived "outsider" (possibly you), you have the potential for disaster. There are some group dynamics that we need to consider. The first is the concept of "diffusion of responsibility". When one person has already committed an act of aggression against a specific target, it's easier for others to follow suit…especially if the target is somehow "different" than the rest of the group. The larger the group, the less responsible any individual within itwill feel. Further, as group members vie for their piece of the action in order to demonstrate their position within the social structure… they are forced to compete with each other in a dangerous game of "one-upsmanship". It would not gain or support status to give a less enthusiastic performance than a compatriot had previously demonstrated. This escalation of hostility can lead a simple misunderstanding into a life-threatening mob attack.

While crimes of social violence may not be as scary on the surface as the asocial predators of the modern lore, they can be just as deadly. Any violent encounter has the potential for accidental injury or to degenerate into a lethal force scenario. In order to recognize the significance of potential threats, it's important to understand something about the common crimes committed during moments of social violence. Here are some of the most common crimes associated with social violence (Legal definitions taken from the POST PC. 832/criminal law and evidence sourcebook):

Assault: (elements) Unlawful attempt coupled with the present ability to commit violence upon the person of another, (class – Misdemeanor)

Basically, if someone demonstrates negative intent toward you via their words or their body language (telling you they are going to hurt you or posturing up) and they are close enough to hurt you (typically invading your personal space)…then they are committing the crime of assault. From a personal protection perspective, if you cannot leave, now is the time to take defensive action.

Battery: (elements) Willful and unlawful use of force or violence upon the person of another, (class – Misdemeanor or Felony if serious bodily injury results)

An easier way of looking at this one is, if someone touches you against your will in an aggressive way…they are committing the crime of battery. This extends to things thrown at or spit on you. I often tell my clients that you do not have to wait to be battered to defend yourself. How often have you heard the old, "I'll let him throw the first punch"? That is SO stupid. What if the first punch knocks you out? What if the first blow wasn't a punch, but it was a knife attack? In real life, you can't afford to that far behind the curve.

Assault With A Deadly Weapon: (elements) Assaults another person with a deadly weapon or instrument, or by means of force likely to cause great bodily injury, (class – Felony)

This means producing a gun, knife, or any other object that would likely kill if it were used against another human being. This statute is purposely vague. The idea is that anything could be used as a deadly implement. A few examples of things that may qualify are hammers, iron pipes, sharp shards, rocks, bricks, sticks, swords, spears, arrows, etc.

Domestic Violence: (elements) Willfully inflicts upon his/her spouse or the mother/father of their child a corporal injury resulting in a traumatic injury, (class – Misdemeanor or Felony if serious bodily injury results)

A sad, but extremely common crime in our society. Essentially, anytime a spouse is physically injured by their significant other, the crime of domestic violence is committed. The primary component here is "corporal injury resulting in a traumatic injury". This could be a simple bruise caused from being grabbed violently by the arm…or severe traumatic wounds from a serious beating.

Terrorist Threats: (elements) Willfully threatens to commit a crime which will result in the death or great bodily injury of another person, thereby causing the victim to be in immediate and/or sustained fear, (class – Misdemeanor or Felony)

People run their mouths all of the time. Hell, it's a free country. We can say anything we want, huh? Nope. Things change when what you say causes someone to fear for their life or the lives of their loved ones. If a person makes a credible/believable threat insinuating that the victim will somehow be in immediate mortal peril…and this causes the victim fear, then the crime of terrorist threats has been committed. An example of a terrorist threat would be if an ex-husband called his estranged wife on the phone and said, "I'm outside the house right now…and I still have a key. I'm coming in there and I'm gonna' slit your throat with one of the kitchen knives." The thing with terrorist threats is they have to be very specific and they must put the victim in immediate and sustained fear.

False Imprisonment: (elements) Unlawful violation of the liberty of another, (class – Misdemeanor or Felony if force, fear or fraud is used)

False imprisonment is the crime of unlawfully holding someone against their will. This can be done merely by intentionally blocking an exit, or as overtly as seizing someone and physically restraining them. If you want to leave, and someone won't let you…chances are, they are committing the crime of false imprisonment.

These are by no means ALL of the crimes committed in the context of social violence, but they are the most common. They appear over and over in a variety of scenarios. Common scenarios of social violence include, but are not limited to, degenerated arguments, status contests, domestic conflicts, vehicular/traffic related conflicts, and workplace hostilities. Knowing the above elements of general crimes-against-persons helps provide some guidelines for appropriate avoidance and response.

Asocial Violence

While social violence is definitely what we most commonly see, what about asocial crime? It may be more rare, but it does exist…and on a significant scale. Unlike social violence, asocial violence does not follow a specific pattern. The asocial attacker's motivations and goals may not be clear or obvious. That's not to say that they don't have specific goals and motivations, simply that they are not going to advertise them to impress members of a social structure. Incidents of asocial violence are mainly the result of predators and occasionally the mentally disturbed.

Perpetrators of asocial violence are the really scary people. They are somehow removed from society and its standard functions. Often times, these people are highly conditioned to violence. They see violence as a tool to be used in the pursuit of their goals. "Normal" people have an inherent aversion to inflicting harm on other human beings. Predators and truly psychotic people don't have that same moral governor. If they do, it's somehow broken. A predator simply sees you as something to exploit, for whatever their purpose.

Again, referencing Rory Miller's classifications, there are two primary types of predators: *resource predators* and *process predators*. Let's talk a little about each. Resource predators, also referred to as "wolves", are bad guys who want something you have…and they are willing to take it using force and/or fear. Examples of resource predators would be armed robbers, carjackers, raiders, etc. Resource predators are referred to as wolves because they behave in similar fashion. They sniff out the weaker prey, and attack at a moment of the prey's disadvantage.

Resource predators actually shop for victims. In interviews that I've personally conducted, and many more that I have read, predators often acknowledge that they are looking for the easy victims. They are not looking for a personal "challenge". They want the quickest easiest means to their end…whatever it is. In many cases, they "audition" potential victims. They will stalk them, canvas their homes, observe their schedules, and more. At the very least, a resource predator is going to chose someone that they feel is physically inferior and unable to withstand an assault. They will not engage if they perceive the risk to be too high.

While we always assume everyone is armed, a resource predator is DEFINITELY armed. Someone who is serious about taking your stuff has probably considered the possibility that you may interfere. As a general rule, these people are career criminals. Career criminals consider weapons tools of the trade. In many cases, they will flash or present their weapon as an intimidation tactic designed to scare you into cooperation. On the good side, if an armed attacker brandishes a weapon and makes demands… they haven't just killed you. It means that they'd prefer you stayed alive, at least for now. From a defensive perspective, this buys you some time.

Another element to consider is that wolves in the wild tend to travel in loose packs. So do some resource predators. In many cases, the locating and exploiting of prey is a joint activity. It's easier to overwhelm a victim both physically and psychologically when there are multiple attackers.

Fortunately, there is one hang up that prevents this from being the standard operating procedure: wolves don't share well. As such, resource predators can see each other as resources and turn on each other. They tend to not trust others…so they often work alone out of necessity.

Resource Predator Pre-assault Indicators:

Inappropriate loitering

A person hanging out in an area that is not socially appropriate is a significant danger sign. For example, a lone man hanging around the women's restroom would be suspicious. If no one comes out to meet him in relative short order, that's not a good sign. Inappropriate loitering is a form of victim shopping. If you notice them, and they notice you…you may have a problem.

Stalking

Someone following you around, particularly in a clandestine manner is a red flag. This is the same behavior a natural predator exhibits right before it pounces on its prey.

Scanning gaze

If someone just starts scanning the area all of a sudden, they are likely checking to ensure that they will be undisturbed in their assault. People say a lot with their eyes.

1,000 yard stare

Speaking of saying a lot with your eyes, the 1,000 yard stare is cold and empty. It seems to look straight through you. That's because it's not looking AT you. The 1,000 yard stare is actually looking over you. By focusing on a point over the target's head and softening the gaze to allow for greater peripheral vision, a predator can effectively scan a wide area for potential interference. This is a more sophisticated version of the scanning gaze, usually performed by an experienced and emotionally removed aggressor. This is a really bad sign.

Prison/gang tattoos

The existence of a prison or gang tattoo does not in and of itself suggest that the person wearing it is about to attack you, but you'd be foolish not to read the writing on the proverbial wall. If someone went through the trouble and the discomfort of getting tattooed in a place you could easily see it, they are probably trying to tell you something. Some tattoos say a whole lot. You'd be well advised to pay attention.

- The "Tear" – Usually indicates that the tattooed party has either raped or killed

- Bars – Inmates often tattoo a jailhouse bars on their bodies to signify the number of years they spent incarcerated

- Elbow spider web – Webs tattooed on the elbows tend to signify time spent behind bars, much the same as the actual bars

- Specific Gang "Tags" – Usually appear as simple letters or graffiti style block letters on the face, neck, or hands

- Skulls and Swastikas - Common in white supremacist and bikergangs

Rapid, direct approach

Someone approaching you with serious negative intent is probably going to do it in a bold movement. When they decide to act, they are not going to waste time. We all know the shortest distance between two points is a straight line. If someone's hurrying right toward you, it may very well be an attack. Recognizing this moment may be the key to avoiding serious harm.

Persistent stranger

What do I mean by the persistent stranger? This is a person who will not go away and leave you alone. Often, their presence was not solicited. They subtly or overtly ignore your desire to be left alone. Someone who is comfortable forcing their presence on others is probably capable of more. They may in fact have a nefarious motive. In his book, <u>The Gift of Fear</u>, Gavin DeBecker uses a perfect example of a persistent stranger. He writes of a true story where a woman has come home from buying groceries. As she unloads her car in the driveway, a man approaches on the sidewalk and offers to help her carry in her groceries. She politely declines, but he ignores her refusal. Eventually, he picks up a bag of groceries and carts it off into her home. She reluctantly follows, and he immediately attacks and brutally rapes her.

6th Sense

This brings us to the next indicator. The woman in the above story commented that she knew something didn't feel right and she was uncomfortable with him entering her home. As a cop and medic, I can't tell you how many times I heard the phrase, "something didn't feel right". LISTEN to your instincts. They don't lie, and they are rarely wrong. If someone suddenly gives you the willies, take it as serious warning sign.

While resource predators commit their crimes for the purpose of acquiring commodities, process predators are all about the act. These are the truly "evil" people. Process predators get off on hurting others. Examples of process predators would be rapists, child molesters, sadists, serial killers, cannibals, etc. These people need to fill some kind of twisted void in their psyche…and you're the fodder. Unfortunately, from a threat recognition perspective, process predators are very difficult to spot. This is primarily because they work very hard to blend in and deceive. Most process predators present themselves under false pretenses, if at all. Some can be disarming and quite charming. When dealing with a process predator, you are often completely unaware until the instant they strike.

Process predators tend to conduct fairly extensive reconnaissance on their potential victims, far more than any other classification of "bad guy". This surveillance is usually conducted at a safe distance and for a period of time. Process predators put a lot of time and energy into their nefarious activities. When they finally get around to the actual attack, they are well prepared. They place you in a situation of disadvantage and then make their move.

The last main category of asocial violent offenders is the mentally disturbed. People with mental health problems fall into this category, not because they are "bad people", but because their behavior does not fall into the scope of normal social aggression. Let's be honest, it gains no social status to go berserk, attacking everyone you see because you believe they are purple aliens coming to steal your soul. It's not always that extreme, but psych patients off their meds can be quite irrational. When an irrational person decides to go violent, all kinds of things can go wrong. The main threat that we need to be concerned with is their enhanced strength.

Having dealt with a lot of these folks from back in my medic days, I can tell you they can become incredibly strong! In many cases, it makes the normal adrenal response seem mild. They rip car doors off, smash metal objects, break their own bones just by stressing out…it's literally crazy! If you see a mentally disturbed individual behaving in an agitated manner, physically avoid them. Feel free to call 911 and get them some help, but don't approach someone in this condition.

Mentally Disturbed Pre-assault Indicators:

Shouting/growling

Highly agitated, mentally disturbed individuals can spout irrational minutia as if it were verbal diarrhea. It may make absolutely no sense, but the tone says everything. If they are hissing and growling their words...look out.

Hyperventilating

In the same context, psychologically disturbed people tend to hyperventilate when very upset. This is the body's attempt to hyper-oxygenate itself. This is a natural biological preparation for battle. Oxygen is a form of fuel, specifically the kind you need a lot of to perform intense physical activity...like combat.

Pacing

When mentally disturbed people pace, it's generally a physical sign of impatience and frustration. They are certainly in an energetic state. The more rapid the pace, the more agitated the individual.

Sudden jerky body movements

For whatever reason, the wiring of their brain/consciousness is different from ours. As such, adrenal stress often manifests itself in odd ways in the mentally disturbed. Body spasms and lurching movements of the core are relatively common signs of impending physical aggression.

Limb flailing

Moving limbs are dangerous limbs, especially when the person wielding them is not all there. If a mentally disturbed person demonstrates this behavior, they are already in an aggressive state. Irrational people often lash out physically at this point, even against people they love and care about.

Slapping themselves/clawing at themselves/pulling their own hair

This is a sign of severe agitation and violent tendencies. They are in such a volatile state, they are literally attacking themselves. A person in this condition is not only a danger to themselves…but anyone around them.

If you're paying attention, the severely mentally disturbed are usually pretty easy to spot and avoid. Unless you are a public safety agent, emergency medical care provider, mental health professional or family member…you should have no need to approach one of these folks. Now, if you do happen to be one of those people who MUST approach dangerous psych patients, seek out specialized training because that is a serious responsibility.

Considering most asocial violence is the work of predators, it's important for us to have a basic grasp of the elements that make up common asocial crimes. What is it that these twisted people are going to try to do to us? Here are some of the crimes-against-persons as outlined in the POST PC. 832/criminal law and evidence sourcebook:

Common Asocial Crimes Against Persons:

Assault With A Deadly Weapon: (elements) Assaults another person with a deadly weapon or instrument, or by means of force likely to cause great bodily injury, (class – Felony)

This does not mean that someone actually has to fire a gun at you or swipe a knife at your throat to commit this crime. If someone raises a gun and points it in your direction, it's reasonable to assume that they are going to kill you. Guns only have one purpose. Likewise, a knife will kill you just the same as a gun. So will getting cracked in the skull with a metal pipe. Anytime someone engages a weapon, it's a safe bet that they are committing this crime.

Mayhem: (elements) unlawfully and maliciously deprives a human being of a member of his/her body or disables, disfigures, or renders it useless, (class – Felony)

Mayhem is a wicked crime. Basically, mayhem is intentionally mangling someone else's body. Shattering bones, ripping someone's eyes out, biting their nose off, dismembering their limbs, genital mutilation…these are all examples of mayhem.

Stalking: (elements) Willfully and repeatedly follows or harasses another person and makes a credible threat with the intent to place the victim in fear, (class – Felony)

This is where things get a little tricky. The crime of stalking encompasses more than someone simply following you around. They have to be persistent and they have to actually threaten you in some way. Now, if a strange guy follows you and you navigate a random course in an attempt to lose him…but he stays with you, you have persistence. That alone isn't stalking. Now, you look over your shoulder and he makes his fingers into a make-shift "gun" and mock fires at you…now he's threatened you too. That would qualify.

Robbery: (elements) Taking of personal property from the person or immediate presence of another, against the will of the victim, and accomplished by means of force or fear, (class –Felony)

In order for the crime of robbery to be committed, the bad guy actually has to take the item from you or your immediate presence. Further, it has to be taken with your knowledge and against your will. For example, I place my wallet on the counter in front of me. A man comes up to me tells me to give him the wallet or he'll beat my ass. I comply and he takes my wallet and leaves. I have just been robbed. Now, same scenario with my wallet on the counter…only this time someone comes up and distracts me, and while I'm distracted, he takes my wallet. Not robbery. That's theft, but not robbery. Robbery requires the use of force or fear.

Carjacking: (elements) Taking a motor vehicle by means of force or fear, (class – Felony)

Carjacking is simply robbery involving a motor vehicle. If someone steals your car in the middle of the night, we have "grand theft auto"… but if someone sticks a gun in your face and takes your car, that's carjacking.

Kidnapping: (elements) uses force or fear to abduct another person against their will, (class –Felony)

I think this one is pretty self explanatory. The main thing to understand with this crime is that abductions don't just occur with little children. People of all ages are abducted for a variety of reasons…none of which are good.

Rape: (elements, abreviated version) the act of sexual intercourse under any of the following circumstances:

- Person is incapable of giving legal consent because of a mental disorder or a physical disability

- Commits against the person's will by means of force, violence, duress, menace, or fear of immediate and unlawful bodily injury on the person of another

- Victim is prevented from resisting by any intoxicating or anesthetic substance or controlled substance, and this condition was known, or should have been known, by the accused.

- Person is unconscious of the nature of the act, and this is known to the accused.

- Person submits under the belief that the person commiting the act is the victim's spouse.

- Accomplished by threats to retaliate in the future against the victim or any other person, and there is a reasonable possibility that the perpatrator will execute the threat.

- Commits against the victim's will by threatening to use the authority of a public official to incarcerate, arrest, or deport the victim or another.

Basically, rape is having sex with someone who is unaware or unwilling. The crime of rape doesn't cover all forms of sexual abuse. There are other sex crimes such as penetration with a foreign object, sodomy, sexual battery, etc. that are just as serious.

> SEX CRIME DATA:
>
> - THE FBI REPORTS THAT 1 IN 3 WOMEN WILL BE SEXUALLY ASSAULTED AT SOME POINT IN THEIR ADULT LIFE.
>
> - ACCORDING TO THE US DOJ, ONE FORCIBLE RAPE OCCURS EVERY 2 MINUTES.
>
> - A NATIONAL CRIME VICTIMIZATION SURVEY CONDUCTED IN 2000 REPORTED THAT 62% OF RAPE VICTIMS KNEW THEIR ASSAILANT.
>
> - THE CURRENT FBI REPORTS SUGGEST THAT THERE IS AT LEAST ONE SEXUAL PREDATOR FOR EVERY SQUARE MILE IN THE CONTINENTAL US
>
> - CHECK WWW.MEGANSLAW.COM FOR A LISTING OF SEXUAL PREDATORS IN YOUR AREA

Homicide: (elements) Killing another person with malice aforethought, (class –Felony)

Essentially this means a person killed someone, and they meant to. In most cases, this is a crime. In all fairness though, there are situations where homicide may be deemed justified. Regardless, asocial criminals won't be using violence in a just manner.

This is just a sampling of the major asocial crimes. Further, each of the above listed crimes has a lot of legal sub-sections.

As asocial violence has a few factors in common, we can at least use the data to recognize some high risk situations. We know that asocial crime is not viewed well by the whole of society. Our current legal structure is designed to apprehend and punish those who commit such acts. As such, criminals are forced to perpetrate their crimes in a clandestine fashion. For this reason, all predators like poorly lit, secluded areas. If predators like it, you should avoid it. Sadly, many enjoyable jogging trails fall into this category.

Resource predators also tend to stalk locations rich in whatever resource they value. In general, this means cash. Walk up ATM's are a biggie. A resource predator knows that the person who just used the ATM probably withdrew money. That doesn't mean they will approach you at the ATM, though they might. They may accost you on the way back to your car or something along those lines. This extends to any kind of regular money transport. Many employers require their employees to make bank runs for the business. Likewise, those who are self-employed find themselves in a similar position. If you transport money, chances are someone knows about it.

Tourist hot-spots are another common "feeding ground". Resource predators know that tourists are probably unfamiliar with the area and consumed by the sights. They also know that touring takes money. If you look like a tourist, you smell like a resource. Shopping malls are another side of the same coin. People who shop need money to buy stuff. If you're a lone shopper, you look like an easy mark. That's why the Holidays are prime crime time.

By recognizing the dynamics of asocial violence and avoiding high risk situations, often times we can negate a problem before it happens. This is actually one of the top 5 bodyguarding rules: "A problem avoided is better than a problem solved". Unfortunately, some threats are persistent and/or difficult to avoid. For this reason, we move into the next segment of the Operational Security Model…the "Personal Perimeter".

Personal Perimeter

I like to think of a personal perimeter as a buffer zone. See danger and avoid it. That's the point of having an effective active scan and good threat recognition skills. The more actual space between you and a potential threat, the better chance you will have of avoiding danger. Space is your friend.

Using the same logic, stationary objects that you can use as practical barriers between you and potential danger are particularly useful. For example, if a guy with a knife is trying to attack you, but there is a car between the two of you, he's going to have a hard time killing you. As long as that vehicle stays in between you and his blade, you're relatively safe. Objects that make good barriers are concrete structures such as pillars or delineators, parked vehicles, commercial mailboxes, heavy furniture, etc. In a pinch, anything is better than nothing. Getting to you should be a challenge for an aggressor.

Staying in motion is another way to maintain space. Also, a moving target is a difficult target. Oftentimes people will physically come to a stop when approached by a stranger. For example, someone passing by asks for the time and the other person stops, looks down at their watch or cell phone, answers the question, and then looks back up. Pretty normal, right? Yeah, well that's also a distraction based ambush. Imagine the same scenario, but this time as our friend looks down at his timepiece… SMACK! Mr. Curious punches the accommodating passer-by in the face, drops him, stomps him a few times, and takes his wallet. If Mr. Helpful had continued walking, kept the stranger in his view as he lifted his watch arm up to his eye line, and answered on the move…an attack would be much more difficult. Don't obediently snap to attention when someone requests your attention. You don't have to be rude, but establish new contacts on your terms.

If there are no objects which can be used as a barrier and motion alone was not enough, then we must use our own body to maintain our personal space. What is "personal space"? Personal space is the area immediately surrounding an individual. On average, most people are comfortable interacting with others at approximately an arm's distance. Invasion of this space is seen as either a hostile or intimate act. Webster's dictionary defines a perimeter as, "the boundary line". Once a threat has approached us, despite our efforts to avoid it, it's time for us to draw a distinct boundary. This is important even in daily life. How many times have you been standing in line at the grocery store, and someone comes up in line behind you and stands right at your heels? We've all had this experience. Most people uncomfortably scootch forward and hope like hell the line moves quickly. Instead, turn around, put your hands up in a conversation posture and politely say, "Oh, excuse me." This places no blame, offers no aggression, but makes it clear you require your personal space.

The adoption of the conversational posture is a universally non-threatening, yet clear setting of a personal boundary. The conversational posture is a position in which the open hands come up, palms out. In assuming this posture it's important to keep the feet about shoulder width apart with a slight bend in the knees to maintain balance. Due to the passive, defensive nature of this motion, it cannot be accidentally perceived as aggression, though it offers significant defensive options. This posture is actually similar to the fighting stance of Muay Thai. From a martial perspective, it's a good defensive position.

Along the same lines, you want to tell any potential witnesses observing this encounter via your body language that you are not the aggressor. In the event you are forced to physically defend yourself, you will want as many witnesses as possible to tell the police that you were attacked, not engaged in mutual combat. If instead of assuming a conversational posture, you balled your fists and put them up like a boxer...or worse yet, jumped into a Karate stance, you would be demonstrating consent to mutual combat. For the record, mutual combat is illegal. It doesn't qualify as self-defense.

Using a passive conversational posture not only prevents escalation and puts witnesses on your side; it can provide an opportunity to verbally diffuse a hostile situation. Almost all violent encounters are preceded by a period of verbal communication. There are, of course, the rare process predators that can attack out of the blue...but they make up a very small percentage those who commit violence against others. As we discussed before, the majority of violent crime is committed in the social setting. ALL social violence involves some kind of pre-assault communication, and most asocial crime does, too. The robber is going to demand your money. That's verbal communication right there.

HOME-BASE PERIMETER MANAGEMENT/SAFETY TIPS:

- LOCK EVERYTHING. INVADERS LIKE AN EASY WAY IN.

- DON'T HIDE KEYS IN COMMONLY USED PLACES OR RIGHT BY THE ENTRY. HIDE THEM IN A TOTALLY SEPARATE PLACE.

- INSTALL HIGH QUALITY DEADBOLT LOCKS.

- REINFORCE YOUR DOOR FRAMES TO ACCOMMODATE A FULL FORCE KICK TO THE DEADBOLT.

- KEEP YOUR SHRUBS AND BUSHES TRIMMED TO MAINTAIN VISIBILITY OUT WINDOWS AND ALONG PATHS.

- KEEP YOUR HOME WELL LIT. MOTION DETECTOR LIGHTING SYSTEMS ARE AFFORDABLE AND EFFECTIVE.

- BUY SECURITY COMPANY STICKERS ON LINE AND PLACE THEM IN YOUR WINDOWS. WHILE YOU MAY NOT BE PAYING FOR A SECURITY SERVICE, CROOKS DON'T KNOW THAT, AND THEY AVOID HOMES THAT LOOK LIKE THEY WILL BE HARD TARGETS.

- LARGE DOGS MAKE EXCELLENT DETERRENTS. THEY BARK WHEN THERE IS AN INTRUDER, AND POSSIBLY EVEN ATTACK THEM FOR YOU.

- HAVE A REHEARSED EXIT PLAN. THINK OF THE FIRE DRILLS YOU DID IN SCHOOL. CREATE AN EVACUATION PLAN FOR YOUR FAMILY, AND THEN TRAIN FOR THE POTENTIAL.

- KEEP A GUN SAFELY SECURED IN THE HOME FOR DEFENSE. BE SURE YOU ARE COMPETENT WITH IT BEFORE YOU RELY ON THE FIREARM AT ALL.

US DOJ DATA REGARDING HOME INVASIONS:

- INVADERS WILL USE EITHER DECEPTION OR OVERWHELMING FORCE TO MAKE ENTRY.

- THERE IS TYPICALLY AN AVERAGE OF 3 ASSAILANTS PER HOME INVASION.

- THEY COMMONLY USE YOUR FAMILY MEMBERS AS HOSTAGES TO LEVERAGE AGAINST YOU.

- 38% OF ASSAULTS AND 60% OF RAPES OCCUR DURING HOME INVASIONS.

- 1 IN 5 US HOMES WILL EXPERIENCE A BREAK-IN OR HOME INVASION.

- THERE ARE OVER 8,000 HOME INVASIONS PER DAY IN NORTH AMERICA

- THERE WAS AN AVERAGE OF 3,600,000 HOME INVASIONS ANNUALLY BETWEEN 1994-2000.

IF SOMEONE BREAKS IN:

- ARM YOURSELF.

- CALL 911, BUT MAKE IT BRIEF.

- GATHER YOUR FAMILY IN THE CLOSEST ROOM WITH AN EXIT (WINDOW, DOOR, SLIDER, ETC.).

- BARRICADE THE DOOR USING WHATEVER YOU CAN FIND.

- GET YOUR FAMILY OUT AND TO A SAFE ZONE.

- IF AN ESCAPE IS NOT POSSIBLE, SET UP A DOOR AMBUSH WHERE YOU WAIT TO ATTACK THEM AS SOON AS THEY BREECH YOUR BARRICADE.

<u>Diffusion and De-escalation</u>

When attempting to verbally de-escalate a situation, it's important that your body language and your vocal tone reflect a condition of non-aggression. It will do you no good to assume a conversational posture and bark out "de-escalation" phrases in a hostile tone. If the two don't match, the situation will escalate. Try to speak in a calm, almost quiet voice. Your gestures and facial expressions should reflect a non-aggressive state. While in this phase, stay hyper-alert. If for some reason things degenerate and you must get physical, at least you will have the element of surprise.

Now, before we get into dealing with other people's behavior, let's not forget ourselves. We are all human, and we all make mistakes. Sometimes we know we screwed up, and sometimes, we don't even realize it. In many cases, a simple apology is the best de-escalation tactic. You don't even have to admit guilt to issue an apology. If someone is upset with you, saying something like, "If I've done something to upset you, I apologize…I don't mean to add difficulty to your day" may off-set the whole thing. Being prepared to accept your share of responsibility for conflict can be very disarming.

Once we've examined ourselves, we can move on to difficult people. Regardless of the nature of the conflict, there are some universal principles to verbally dealing with difficult people. Dr. George J. Thompson goes into great depth on the subject in his book <u>Verbal Judo – The Art of Persuasion</u>. Much of what I share with you here is based on his work. If you have not read his text, it's a must.

The first principle that we need to embrace is empathy. To empathize with someone does not mean to take their side or agree with them in any way. It simply means that you look at things from their perspective. Try to understand what they are thinking, feeling, and what they want. If you understand something about their motivations, you will have a tactical advantage. Be observant and listen to what they say. In a lot of cases, as they rant, they tell you what the solution to the problem is.

People can become so upset that they lose sight of their own goals. They get so caught up in the anger and heat of the moment, common sense goes out the window. If you can maintain enough presence of mind to recognize these moments and bring an aggressor back to their true goals, you may be able to avert violence.

The next principle to successful diffusion is never verbally challenging someone in the middle of a conflict. Forcing someone to rise to your challenge is an act of escalation, not de-escalation. Challenges are designed to provoke another into action. Don't knowingly add fuel to a fire. Further, by challenging someone, you may entice them to act more harshly than they had intended. Perhaps they weren't going to hit you until you said, "I dare you...you just try and hit me."

Another key principle is never to threaten. Issuing threats in the middle of a conflict is foolish. First of all, if you issue a threat, you place yourself in the position of A) having to make good on the threat, or B) having to back down when your bluff is called...losing you ground. Neither of these things do anything to de-escalate a volatile situation. Also, you demonstrate an attitude of aggression that may cause them to behave in a more aggressive manner than before. If you're aggressive, they must be MORE aggressive to maintain their position in the altercation.

Along the same lines, barking orders at someone you're trying to avoid physical conflict with is a bad idea. Cops do this a lot, and many times, it gets them knee deep in a brawl. Don't issue commands. No one likes to be told what to do. It makes people mad. Obviously, if it makes folks mad, it's probably not something you want to do to someone you're trying to calm down. A better idea is to offer suggestions. If there is something you want your aggressor to do, set it up in such a way he feels like he's choosing to do that thing of his own accord. For example, instead of telling a panhandler to go away...suggest he try the parking lot across the street.

Never insinuate that they are wrong. Telling someone that they are wrong will only upset them and escalate a touchy situation. Instead, present evidence to sway their opinion. If it's really not important, let them be "right". Insinuating that someone is wrong can often be taken as a challenge. We have already discussed how well a challenge is received during verbal conflict.

If at all possible, it's incredibly helpful to leave them a face-saving exit. An aggressor is far more likely to peacefully disengage if he thinks he will not lose status as a result. If there is a possibility that he will look like a coward or the loser, the odds of him leaving peacefully are low. If an aggressor can walk away the victor or at least having lost nothing, the odds of a peaceful resolution go way up. For example, if a guy gets in your face and postures up, and you tell him you don't want to fight him because he seems really tough…he may very well have just received what he wanted. He didn't have to fight you to gain the status of being viewed as a badass; you just gave it to him. He can walk away and lose no face in front of his buddies, his girl, or his gang. This is a win-win. He gets his empty status, and you don't get hurt.

There are those who say, "Oh, this de-escalation crap is bullshit. Leave him a face-saving exit! I'll just wreck the dude. Better to be tried by 12 than carried by 6." Well that's fine and good, and when the rubber meets the road, I agree with the "fight now and sort the rest out later" concept…but there is the smart way to manage threats and there's also the way that gets you thrown in prison. We live in a nation of laws, and unless you want to spend the rest of your life behind bars over some idiot, I think it's best to learn to use your words as a shield. Put your ego away during conflict. Feel pride that you can keep your calm and out-think the aggressor.

Which brings me to the final principle in the progression, let them have the last word…you get the last act. Everyone seems to need to get in the last word, as if that signifies that they "win". Let them. By choosing not to pursue the matter further, you get to take the final act of leaving. What are more powerful, words or actions? Actions are. A politician can tell you how great things will be under his administration, but until actions are taken…none of the talk matters. When you take action, you take control. What they say doesn't matter as much as what you do.

Well, all of this sounds great in theory, but what about when the pressure actually comes? What about when they start spouting horrible profanities and insults in your direction? That's distracting, uncomfortable, and possibly overwhelming. If you don't have a pre-planned method of disarming insults, you are going to be in a difficult psychological position.

Before we can create a plan to circumvent insults, we need to understand what they are and where they come from. What are insults? Insults are verbal jabs designed to break you mentally. Think about that. They are mere words meant to break you. I don't know about you, but I'm not that fragile. Someone calling me a name or cursing at me is not going to have a lasting impact my self esteem. I don't give them that power. First of all, they probably don't even know you. Even if they do, chances are that they are not that important to you. How much can their insults really mean? In the event someone you care about is insulting you, you may want to re-evaluate that relationship. Perhaps the relationship needs counseling…or perhaps it's not what you think it is. Keep in mind what an insult is. Someone who cares about you doesn't want to break you.

When insults are slung your way, we can deflect and by-pass them using a verbal countermeasure Dr. Thompson refers to as a "strip phrase". A strip phrase is a brief acknowledgement of their jab, but one that offers no emotional investment. For example, when insulted, responding with a drawn out, "Ahhhh Yessss…but…", or, "Riiiight…" can effectively address and neutralize the offense. If they are really persistent with their verbal assault using the strip phrase, "I understand that you're really upset" is a great response. Using a strip phrase not only provides you a response, it also serves to disempower the aggressor. When his insults don't have the desired effect, in a way, he becomes psychologically impotent.

Aside from simply deflecting insults, we need to take an active role in de-escalation hostilities. There are several very effective de-escalation tactics you may wish to employ. Depending on your personality and the situation you find yourself in, you may wish to use one or more of the following:

De-escalation Tactics:

Deflection –

Deflection is the act of bouncing aggression off of you, and placing the mess back in their lap. People are selfish. They don't care about you. Make it about them. Making a comment like, "I'm sorry you're having a rough day" reminds them that their issues are not necessarily with you. If someone is extremely hostile with you, odds are they are mad for other reasons. You just happen to be the convenient outlet.

Rationally Negotiate –

In most situations, a cool head will prevail. If you can find a solution that works for everyone…yeah-hoo! In the midst of a heated argument, it is possible to offer a compromise or accommodation that works for everyone. The key to conflict resolution is LISTENING to what the other person is saying. Again, empathize. Put yourself in their position. What is it that they want? Can you give it to them? If not, can you suggest another way they could get what they need? Negotiation doesn't mean surrender, rather finding an equitable solution.

Question –

If the verbal conflict appears to be deadlocked and going nowhere, ask them, "What's your goal here?" Perhaps they have lost sight of that as well. When people are angry, they can get carried away and forget everything but the emotion. Be direct. Ask, "How can we solve this problem"? They may give you the answer. In your own emotional confusion, perhaps it eluded you.

Humor –

Perhaps one of the most disarming strategies is humor. My friend, Richard Dimitri, tells a story about a guy who approached him all pissed off. The guy gives Rich a hard look and asked, "You got a fuckin' problem?!" Rich chuckled and responded with, "Yeah brother. I've got a lotta' problems" Then he laughed and continued with, "…none with you though. Why? Does it show on my face?" The aggressor was kind of thrown off guard, but as Rich was laughing, he laughed back, gave a half-ass response and moved along. It's tough to be mad at someone who's making you laugh. Now, Rich is pretty quick and sharp witted. If you don't have a great sense of humor, or you don't feel particularly witty…perhaps this one is not for you. However, if you have the ability, use it.

Remove Self from Hierarchy –

Especially when dealing with conflicts over social status, aggressors tend to select people they think fall into their hierarchy. A good example is the young macho male crowd. They will play testosterone games with any man who wants to participate for status, but they tend to focus on men they see as potential rivals. If you make it known that you are not a member of this community, they may very well lose interest. For example, if your hair is going a little grey you can use the line (in a non-patronizing tone), "Look, I'm old enough to be your dad.

I don't want to compete with you, son." You don't have to say, "I'm a wimp. You'd kill me in a fight". Just excuse yourself from the running for "top macho alpha dog".

Distract –

An effective distraction takes their mind off of their current point of focus, and places their attention elsewhere. For example, if someone is yelling at you and invading your personal space and you point out that someone behind them is dialing their cell phone with intent, if you tell them that you believe that person is calling the police, their attention will shift back to their well being. Again, people are selfish. Make them consider their situation. Another example would be if a man coming out of a store with his family suddenly became aggressive toward you. Pointing out that his child seems scared and that you understand why he needs to tend to his family may switch his thought patterns. The idea is to make them consider something else that matters to them.

Raise Stakes –

Another tactic is to raise the stakes. Sure, this situation is bad, but it could be worse. Explain why this is bad for both of you. Remember not to threaten. Saying something like, "Oh, YOU'RE in trouble now. Do YOU want to go to jail?" may prompt a response of resolve and courage. They may say, "I've been there. I ain't scared!" Now they have committed to the bitter end. I guarantee you; they don't want to go to jail. Instead say something like, "Hey man, I don't want to go to jail, do you? I just want to leave before the cops get here." This insinuates that the situation can deteriorate further…and they have a choice. Once the reminder of jail comes up, perhaps they find a way to excuse themselves without losing face rather than get violent.

In order to effectively employ these diffusion and de-escalation tactics, we need to be familiar with the various psychological aggressor profiles we may face during conflict. Each has a different goal, and each requires a different response in order to diffuse their aggression. Now, in fairness, there is no guarantee when it comes to reading people, but there are some commonalities that offer a good starting point.

General Aggressor Profiles – Social Violence:

Temporarily Stupid –

Social violence is often perpetrated not by the proverbial "bad guy", but by a "temporarily stupid" individual. I know, it's a great term. Someone who is temporarily stupid is generally a non-criminal, who for whatever reason, decides to behave like a jackass. Some examples of things that can drive regular folks to behave badly are alcohol, drugs, or lack of meds, loss of a job, relationship problems, unusually high stress, etc. People from all walks of life can become temporarily stupid. Under different circumstances, you may even have liked this person.

In many cases, we may know the person. Perhaps they are a coworker or an acquaintance. The best way to keep people you know from feeling like they can "dump" on you when they are having a bad day is to command respect. In order to do this, you must carry yourself with confidence and address all breeches of respect. For example, most folks do not verbally object when teased or harassed. If something bothers you, you should. You don't have to be hostile or rude, but letting people know where your lines are demonstrates confidence and self-esteem. Consider this; there are three guys working in the same office, Sam, George, and Bill. Bill is a mild mannered guy, kind of quiet, and he keeps to himself. When he's upset, he broods at his desk. George is a fun, outgoing guy who always speaks what's on his mind. Agree or disagree, you can count on George to speak up. If there's a problem, George wants to solve it...and he'll get involved. Sam's an ass. He's rude and aggressive. When Sam has a bad day, who do you think he takes it out on…George or Bill? Right, Bill. Bill is the easy mark. Don't be that easy mark.

So, when someone is temporarily stupid and giving you grief, what do you do? The best answer is, in a calm quiet voice, politely point out their inappropriate behavior and explain that you don't wish to engage in hostilities with them. Deflecting and questioning tactics can be particularly useful with these people. They are often distraught over something else entirely. Bringing them back to the root of their issue often switches their focus off of you and back onto their own life problems.

Territorial –

This is a natural behavior in all animals. My guess is you are territorial too. Wouldn't you take offense to someone walking into your home unannounced and eating their sack lunch at your table? Of course you would. Hell, they might be quickly introduced to the resident shotgun. Well, other people are territorial too. The issue comes in when someone feels that you have violated their territory or are trespassing on their "turf".

The claims people make on territory are not always valid. For example, if you are at a public bus stop and some gangbanger takes offense at your presence because he thinks that his gang owns the whole city… it's tough to buy into that. The important thing is HE buys into that. He believes that this is HIS property, and you are trespassing. A person defending their territory is extremely dangerous. People get killed over park benches. In many cases there is more at stake than just your individual encounter. In their mind, they need to send a clear message to anyone who would violate their space. If they don't deal with you decisively, their claim could soon be threatened by other groups that perceive them as weak.

When dealing with territorially aggressive people, make it known you respect their claim. If you can, leave. Find other transportation, take another route, go to a store and call someone…but leave. If you cannot leave, explain why you need to pass through and that you intend no aggression. When I used to live in Sothern California, I had to walk my little girl to her school and navigate through my neighborhood. It was a tough neighborhood and there were several gangs. Once I realized that regardless of which route I selected, we'd have to pass through a gang infested area, I decided to pre-emptively approach the local gangbangers I'd later see with my daughter. As soon as I approached their group, they hopped off their car bumpers and headed toward me. Right away I assumed a conversational posture and introduced myself. They asked me what I was doing in their "hood", clearly ready to show my little white ass that I was in the wrong place. I told them that I lived in the neighborhood, and that I understood what was going on. I also told them that I respected their guard duty, that I was glad that they were looking out for the neighborhood, because my family and I lived there too. I asked them if they had kids, and several of them said they did. I explained that I'm not a hard-core gangbanger badass like them; I'm just a daddy that has to walk his little girl from the front door to school and home. Their tone changed, they started calling me "hommie" and suggested that they respected my attitude and that I was welcome to pass through with my daughter anytime. From then on, anytime I passed by it was always, "Hey, what's up hommie!" Show respect and explain yourself, it goes a long way. And, for what it's worth, I moved my family out of that neighborhood as fast as I could!

Physically Aggressive –

This one is so common, especially among males in their late teens through their thirties. Men seem to operate on a very primitive model. We look to establish dominance in our respective hierarchies by demonstrating aggressive behavior. This position is promoted in the movies and television shows we watch. Our heroes are all really good at beating people up. If you can whoop someone's butt, you're a man, damn it. Further, other personality profiles can degenerate into this state if they feel challenged in some way.

The physically aggressive assailant is looking to gain social standing, teach you a lesson, or enforce his territorial demands. All of these boil down to the fact that he's trying to establish alpha status. If you want to de-escalate a conflict with someone in this position, give them what they want. Acknowledge their alpha status. I like to use the phrase, "Hey, you're obviously a tough guy…I don't want to fight with you." In that simple response I publicly give him alpha status. From a psychological perspective, I lose nothing. I didn't say I'm not tough. I just acknowledged that he was tough too. As Brazilian/Gracie Jiu-jitsu Master Rickson Gracie says, "Tough guys grow on trees…you can find them anywhere". There is no shame in acknowledging that another guy seems tough.

You can also demonstrate that there is no status to be gained by fighting with you. I'm a small person. I'm 5'8" and I only weigh only around 140 lbs. Now, I may have a lifetime of martial training under my belt, but at first glance, I'm pretty unassuming. In order to show them that there is no status to be gained by hurting me, I make comments like, "Look, you're twice my size. Kicking my ass would prove nothing… except that you're twice my size". Often, that's enough to convince them that the possible consequences aren't worth the gain.

Sexually Aggressive –

In our society, we promote to our young men that sexually aggressive behavior wins female favor. After all, women play hard to get and it's the persistent guy that prevails, right? That's not necessarily reality, but that is a common view held by many men. In many situations, males will make overt sexual overtures at lone women, groups of women, women travelling with a male companion, and even other males. There's hooting and whistling, "Hey baby…" lines, blatant sexual commentary, and lewd behavior. Generally speaking, this type of attention is not appreciated.

While some self defense instructors say that it's best to ignore this kind of behavior, I have to disagree. By ignoring it, you passively condone it, and you give them the opportunity to escalate the encounter. Verbally acknowledge their dishonorable behavior. This can be done by inserting a strip phrase like, "Riiiiight". This tells them you heard them, and you don't approve…but it is non-inflammatory. If you are a female being accosted, let them know in no uncertain terms that you are not interested. Be very clear. Don't expect a sexually aggressive male to "take a hint". As soon as possible, leave.

If you are a male escorting a female companion, and a sexually aggressive male makes an overture at your lady friend, it is not only a sign of sexual interest…it's also an act of primal aggression against you. It's a challenge. Your initial instinct is probably to jump on the dude and pound his face into mud. This is probably not a good idea. While third party protection tactics exceed the scope of this manual, I will say that your primary responsibility at this point is to get her to a safer place, not issue an "educational beatdown" to the jackass. Don't stop and have a "moment" with them. Remember our rule about people having friends? He may be one of several assailants preparing to ambush the two of you.

Opportunistic Bully –

This type of aggressor is someone who takes advantages of you at a moment of perceived weakness in order to make themselves look or feel better. Often done under the guise of "friendly teasing", an opportunistic bully may insult you, poke fun at you, tell offensive jokes in your presence, play pranks on you, or any of the like. Remember our concept of commanding respect? Call them on their inappropriate behavior. Ask them to put themselves in your place. Explain that this behavior creates an adversarial condition, and you'd rather get along. In many cases, if you show them respect and then explain that you require it back…you gain their cooperation.

If they are not interested in what you have to say because they now perceive you as prey, enlist social assistance. In general, bullying is done in front of an audience. If no one sees how much "cooler" they are then you, then little is accomplished. We've all been in one of those situations where someone was giving someone else a hard time. We didn't think it was cool, but we nervously giggled and exchanged uncomfortable glances. In some cases, people actually laugh out loud and begin to participate. This comes down to a concept known as "diffusion of responsibility". When one person behaves in a questionable manner, others may participate simply because it seems to be accepted. The more people participating, the easier it is for people to justify and excuse their actions. They may also see someone else on the attack and rather than end up on the receiving end, they join in. Before the crowd turns on you, enlist their help. By making direct eye contact or pointing at an individual, you single them out of a crowd. This removes them from the security of group behavior, and makes them personally accountable. Ask them how they'd feel if someone treated them in this fashion. Typically, they respond by saying that they would not appreciate that kind of treatment. This demonstrates to the bully that this behavior doesn't gain social standing with this group. This is a technique I teach to children for managing bullies, as it works well.

Hustler –

These are the underhanded, self-serving, manipulative types that want to use you for their purposes and screw you out of whatever they can. They will pretend to be your ally to take advantage of you. In fact, they use specific psychological tricks to make you believe they are somehow joined to you. Using manipulations such as forced teaming, where a person use words like, "us" and "we" to insinuate that the two of you are linked in some way, is a common strategy to reel you in. Here's an example of an actual hustle; while waiting in line at the bank, the guy in front of you sparks up a conversation. "Look at us", he says.

'We've been standing here waiting forever. We have stuff to do. I have to get to my son's birthday party…and I barely have enough time to pick up his present. I need my money to go get his present". Looking at you he says, "I bet you have kids". You say yes, and the two of you talk about parenthood and how much you love your children. As the line progresses, he goes up to the next available bank teller and you head to another. You conduct your business, but as soon as you are done, your new "friend" approaches you. He tells you that the teller told him he can't access his money because the checks he deposited haven't cleared yet. You, of course, know how important a child's birthday is, so your "friend" asks you to loan him a little money. After all, he's an honorable father desperate to be there for his child, right? In fact, he tells you that if you give him your address, he'll mail it back to you. Don't buy it.

A hustler may also do something to make you feel indebted, and then try to extort something from you. If someone is always providing unsolicited favors, be cautious. Don't trust people you don't know. If something seems too good to be true, it probably is. People rarely ever give anything with no expectation of return. It's just a sad fact.

The best way to avoid being taken advantage of by a hustler is to express independence. By making it known that you are comfortable and capable of handling things on your own, they become unnecessary. You don't have to be rude, but when someone insists on "helping" you, tell them, "No thank you. I like to do things for myself. It makes me feel good about myself". If someone tries to take advantage of you because you are in some kind of trouble, tell them, "I appreciate your attempt to help, but I got myself into this, and I'll get myself out. I just need to figure things out for myself. Thanks."

General Aggressor Profiles – Asocial Violence:

It's important to understand something about an aggressor's psychological condition. Resource predators engage in a high risk situation every time they commit a crime. There is a lot of adrenaline happening there, on both sides. Sure, you're scared…but he's jacked up and adrenalized. Also, a lot of resource predators have serious drug addictions; that in and of itself can make a person unstable. He may also be very nervous. Some criminals panic under the stress of their own actions. The point is, don't expect a wolf to be a calm, cool customer.

Trying to verbally de-escalate a social conflict is difficult enough, but diffusing an asocial aggressor, that's a whole other ball game. Asocial aggressors are far more unpredictable and volatile. Understanding that it is unlikely these types of aggressors will just leave us alone with a little verbal encouragement, a diffusion attempt is still worth the effort because anything we can do to avert violence is in our best interest. Worst case scenario, it doesn't work. If that is the end result, we've lost nothing.

First, let's talk about the resource predators. They tend to be some form of robber. A robber has a very specific agenda. He wants your property, and he's going to take it…by force if necessary. In this case, de-escalating the situation means calming him from his adrenalized state to a calmer more rational one. The more nervous and agitated a robber, the more likely he is to commit violence. If someone sticks a gun or knife in your face and demands your stuff, give it to them. Don't get mouthy or hostile. It may be tempting, but it will only escalate a bad situation with an unstable person. Even if you can disarm and beat up this bad guy, you may sustain major injuries in the process. Perhaps some other innocent bystander gets wounded. Better to let them take the property and deal with the aftermath later. Now, if they demand more than property…no deal.

I tend to break down process predators into two main categories, **rapists** and **killers**. As both have different goals, your de-escalation tactics should account for this. When dealing with rapists, they have a general verbal pattern they follow. This pattern was initially presented by Special Agent Robert Hazelwood, Behavioral Science Instruction/Research Unit, Quantico, VA. in his paper, "The Criminal Behavior of the Serial Rapist".

Rapist verbal pattern –

Orders

This is the most common verbal communication made by a would be rapist. They begin by giving directives like, "Shut up", "Take off your clothes", or "Get down on the floor." Don't comply. This only ensures that you will be taken advantage of. Calmly tell them that you will not participate. Make it clear that this is very much against your wishes. Every situation is different, but sometimes you may sense an opportunity to reach them on some level. Perhaps you can offer a face-saving exit, for example, "You're a big, strong guy. While I don't want to have sex with you, there are plenty of women who would be happy to hook up. You don't need to do this."

Threats

If you fail to obey their orders, they usually move to making threats. Threats can include verbal threats and insinuated threats. They may tell you that they will kill you, or hurt your loved ones. They may not say anything. If you tell a rapist that you won't cooperate, and he balls up a fists, raises his hand, and gives you a hard stare…that's an insinuated threat. Threats are to be taken seriously. In many cases, at this point, things have become physical. At this point, "raising the stakes" and reminding them of the consequences of their actions may be appropriate.

Negotiation

When a victim is uncooperative, and the aggressor is hesitant to get too physical, they may start to negotiate. Negotiations work something like this, "Look, I was gonna' choke you out, tie you up, and ass rape you... but, if just let me have regular sex with you, I'll leave". This shows that if you decide to concede, things will go easier for you. This is a lie. Your negotiating chips are things like, "I won't call the cops if you leave now" (you're lying, of course), or "I'll talk to some friends about you". Understand that once the "bad stuff" starts...it only escalates until they have completed their fantasy. Who knows, they may plan to kill you when they finish. Maybe that's part of the fantasy. You don't know. There are some sick folks out there! Don't comply.

This brings us to the killers. It takes a very rare personality to truly be okay killing another human being. It takes an even more rare individual to enjoy killing. To be honest, you are unlikely to verbally dissuade a killer from acting on his impulse, but when your life is on the line, it's worth a shot. Your first, best option is to find a way to "humanize" yourself. In order to kill you, they have to view you as "less than human". They have psychologically removed themselves from you. You need to find a way to relate to them in a way that appeals to them. Empathize. Calmly try to show them that you are a person like them. It's much harder to kill someone you have an affinity for.

In the process of "befriending" your attacker, don't give up any personal or health information. For example, if you notice your attacker has a leg wound, don't tell the killer that your leg is wounded too. He'll use that against you. Likewise, don't say something like, "Please don't kill me. I have a five year old daughter". They may try and use your child against you. Keep it simple. In this instance, it's okay to lie. Pretend.

Mentally Disturbed –

The mentally disturbed may or may not be criminal, but they are definitely a factor to consider when talking about asocial violence. When a mentally disturbed person becomes a danger to themselves and others, there is a safety code that allows medical professionals and police officers to place a disturbed individual in protective custody for almost 3 days. This "5150" action, as it was known back in my law enforcement days, is a provision designed to protect the public and the mentally ill person. In many cases, an altered level of consciousness is due to a medical condition such as a diabetic emergency, a schizophrenic episode, Alzheimer's based dementia, and the like.

An altered level of consciousness can also be the result of chemical influence. Drugs and alcohol can have profound impacts on the brain. Chemical influences can cause hallucinations, delusions, paranoia, anxiety, and much more.

Psychological stress is another potential factor in mental health emergencies. Situations where people are exposed to moments of extreme psychological stress such as the death of a loved one, a mortally close call, a PTSD trigger, or some other personal burden can result in a nervous breakdown. When this happens, they become completely unstable and unpredictable.

When trying to diffuse a hostile encounter with a mentally disturbed individual, what you say isn't as important as how you say it. Speak in a calm, quiet voice. Use slow, non-aggressive movements. The conversational posture works well here. Do your best to tell them that you want to get them some help. This not only tells them you are not an aggressor; it also gives you an excuse to leave. If they are incoherent or irrational, play into their delusion. Don't try and tell them they are wrong. Remember from our earlier de-escalation training that telling someone they are wrong is inflammatory. If they think you are the purple alien people, explain that the purple alien people are good. Tell them you are going to find someone to help explain everything. Don't try to "snap them back into the real world".

If despite your efforts to calm them, they continue to become violent, change your tone to a loud aggressive one and yell at them to get back at the top of your lungs. Sometimes, this is a shock to their nervous system and they briefly withdrawal back into themselves. This, of course, is a last ditch effort, as yelling straight away is a great way to get a mentally disturbed person riled up.

Defensive Countermeasures

If our verbal attempts fail, or there is no opportunity for communication, our only recourse is violence of action. That's why we have defensive countermeasures. If it becomes necessary to use violence in self-defense, we need to be sure that our actions are not only effective, but that they fall within legal parameters. This really should not be a problem, because the law allows for reasonable force…all the way up to lethal force in appropriate situations.

That being said, self-defense is a unique defensive strategy in today's legal system. Claiming self defense in court carries several ramifications. The claim of self-defense is considered an "Affirmative Defense". This means that you openly acknowledge that you hurt another person on purpose. If you somehow fail to prove that your actions legally qualify as self-defense, you have already admitted guilt. Further, the burden of proof is now on the defense…YOU.

If you claim self defense, you must be prepared to explain why all other choices were worse. Violence is a last resort option as far as the law is concerned. One of the first questions they will ask you in court is, "why didn't you just leave"? If this was an argument over ego, and you felt the need to stick around until you "won"…that's no longer self-defense. For example, a guy across the street yells a profanity at you. You say, "What did you say?" and stop and wait for him to cross the street. You stand there dumbfounded with your arms out at your sides in a gesture of "what the hell"? He repeats his curse, and you punch him in the face. You may have felt like you did the right thing, but in court later, they're going to ask why you couldn't have just walked away when he first issued the curse. Chances are, you're going to lose your self-defense case.

Keep in mind that just because you can do something, doesn't mean you must. While a situation may provide you the legal right to use force, you may decide that's not your best option. Perhaps you are having success talking them down, maybe they are very young, perhaps this is your child or a loved one…the bottom line is you are not a police officer obligated to act. You have the choice.

Further, if you have to use violence, the law requires you to use the minimum level of force that you reasonably believe is necessary to safely resolve the situation. Now, what's "reasonable" is very subjective. After the fact, other people will arm-chair quarterback your behavior in a calm, sterile environment. In this environment, any violent act seems magnified. They won't have to deal with any of the adrenal stress or split-second decisions you did. But, they will decide if what you did was "reasonable". A good rule to follow is, "Do only what you must to stop the threat…and then stop immediately." Once you are "safe", anything more makes you an aggressor in the eyes of the law.

This is important because you can begin a situation completely the defender, and end up in a pair of handcuffs for going too far. For example, many traditional martial arts offer "self-defense progressions" that go something like this: "Block an incoming strike, punch to the throat, sweep the attacker to the ground, chop to throat, stomp to rib cage, and step back into stance." If this was a situation of social violence where one man punched another during an argument, and the "defender" crippled the initial aggressor…the defender has now become the aggressor, and he's definitely going to jail. Two strikes to the throat and a body stomp to a downed assailant may even qualify as lethal force. The countervailing force must be appropriate to the attack. If someone pushes you, you can't Karate chop them in the throat and collapse their trachea.

So, how are you supposed to know how much force to use? To answer that question, you first must know your options. Police officers are required to follow a use-of-force policy that is approved by their department. As a civilian, you don't answer to a departmental chain of command, but you are bound by the same legal system. It is in your best interest to develop and adhere to your own use-of-force policy. Because you're a civilian, your use-of-force policy should reflect this. You don't carry 25 lbs. of law enforcement gear around with you everywhere you go. Chances are, you don't cruise around in body armor either. You don't have a radio equipped with an emergency button to access an entire department of cops the instant your butt is in a bind. You also don't have any duties or responsibilities to play superhero. As such, your use-of-force policy should focus on escape and evasion, rather than confrontational combatives.

Use-of-Force

I was recently exposed to the Canadian "Circle-chart" model used to represent the use-of-force options. I like this model the best out of all I have come across. Generally, the use-of-force policy has been represented as a ladder, requiring the user to take each step in progression before moving on. This is great in theory, but in practice, there are times you need to skip wrungs on the ladder. The circle chart model allows the individual to choose which of the options is most appropriate at the moment. I have modified the law enforcement circle chart to reflect the needs of the civilian (see Figure 1).

Let's discuss each of these Use-of-Force Options:

Presence

When you perceive suspicious behavior, but no laws have yet been broken, assume a confident posture. Make it clear that you are aware of your surroundings and their presence. Do not provoke them or try to stare them down, just be alert and on the move.

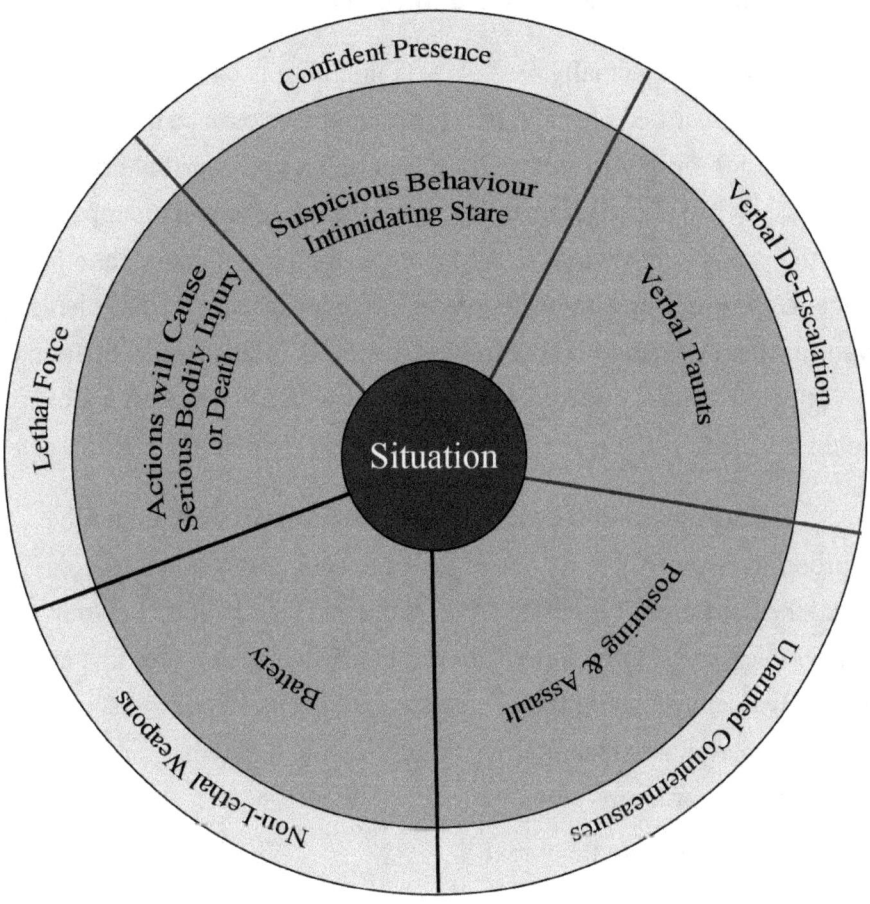

Figure 1

Verbal De-escalation/Conflict Resolution

When confronted with verbal aggression, the appropriate course of action is to try to verbally diffuse the hostility. The law doesn't consider it self-defense if you get physical with someone who insults you. For advice in this department, refer to the above section on de-escalation.

Empty-Hand, Non-lethal Physical Intervention

If someone actually assaults you or commits battery against you, you can use unarmed physical fighting techniques to make them stop. This does not mean you must wait to be struck or physically hurt before you act in self-defense. Remember, assault is an unlawful attempt coupled with the present ability to commit violence upon the person of another. If someone postures up and invades your personal space, you don't have to wait for them to batter you before you respond. In fact, you'd be foolish to. The first strike could knock you out…or worse yet, the fist could be holding a blade you were unaware of. Don't wait to be injured.

That being said, the techniques you use have to fall under the appropriate use-of-force parameters. If they collapse as soon as you strike them, you can't jump on top of them and start beating on your fallen adversary. Further, there are some unarmed techniques that are generally deemed "lethal force" maneuvers in court. Here are some common martial arts techniques that have resulted in lethal force and been prosecuted accordingly:

Open hand chops to the throat

Punches to the throat

Knee strikes to the back of the head

Knee strike to the temple

Knee strikes to the cervical vertebrae

Kicks to the head of a fallen foe

Kicks to the neck/throat of a fallen foe

Stomps to the head of a fallen foe

Stomps to the chest

Stomps to the abdomen

Stomps to the spine

Intentionally smacking the skull into hard surfaces

Note: Lethal force is a force option, but it's not this one. If and when we deem lethal force necessary, any of these techniques would then become "fair game".

Non-lethal weapons

In my opinion, this area doesn't have much to offer civilians. Impact weapons, such as kubotans and expandable Asp batons are sold to the general public, but they require a fair amount of training to use effectively. Also, in the case of kubatons, they usually attach to a key ring. You will likely need your keys to make your escape. When fighting with a small impact tool such as a kubaton, they tend to fall out of your grasp upon significant impact. This can be problematic if it places your keys out of reach.

Another common self defense suggestion that deals with keys is the placing of keys between the digits and making a "spiked" fist. This is so foolish. Don't do this! First of all, the keys will lacerate your fingers upon impact, probably making you drop them. Also, each key will have a different contact point. When you hit someone, one key will go one direction while other keys move in random directions. Often, this causes dislocations of the knuckles and fractures of the phalanges. Essentially, it's a good way to mangle your hand.

As far as OC and pepper sprays go, I don't advocate those at all. All spray systems have back spray or mist that can affect you too. Further, it's unreliable. In police academy, the training staff sprayed each of us with law enforcement grade OC…directly in the face. Half the class had snot and tears running all over the place. A few threw up. There was also about a third of the class that didn't seem to care too much. If you happen to be one of the sensitive folks, and your attacker is resilient… using a chemical agent could be worse for you than for them. Even if he does respond horribly to be being sprayed, that may not stop him from clinching with you. If this happens, you'll likely be contaminated and possibly overcome as well. In law enforcement training, officers are taught to use their impact weapon in conjunction with OC spray. The idea is to spray the offender, and then keep him away from you now that he's contaminated.

> **REALITY CHECK:** AS CORRECTIONAL OFFICERS ARE NOT ALLOWED TO CARRY FIREARMS WITHIN THE PRISON OR JAIL FACILITY, THE PRIMARY WEAPON USED TO MAINTAIN ORDER AND SUBDUE HOSTILE INMATES IS OC SPRAY. AS SUCH, MANY INMATES TAKE MEASURES TO IMMUNIZE THEMSELVES TO THE EFFECTS OF LAW ENFORCEMENT GRADE OC/PEPPER SPRAYS. ONE OF THE WAYS THEY DO THIS IS TO TAKE PEPPER PACKETS FROM THEIR COMMISSARY AND RUB THE CONTENTS DIRECTLY INTO THEIR EYES. EVENTUALLY, THEY CONDITION THEMSELVES TO THE PAIN AND SENSATIONS THAT ACCOMPANY AN OC VOLLEY.

If you're going to carry a non-lethal weapon, I suggest a taser. Not a stun-gun or a "zapper"…I mean an actual taser, like the X26. These hand held tasers shoot dart cartridges that deliver high voltage stuns. They are extremely effective, provided you are accurate enough to hit the target. The big downsides are you only get one shot…and they are pricey.

Lethal force

Lethal force is a level of response likely to kill. This includes the unarmed skills mentioned in the above section, hitting someone in the head with a heavy object, stabbing someone, shooting someone, etc. If you are attacked in a manner likely to cause serious bodily injury or death to you or another, the law authorizes the use of deadly force.

Likewise, sexual assaults (rape, forced oral copulation, sodomy, penetration with a foreign object, etc.) also justify the use of lethal force. Sexual violation is considered "serious bodily injury" and warrants an extreme defensive response. Keep in mind, aside from the obvious trauma of a sexual assault, sexually transmitted diseases can be deadly. You have no way of knowing whether or not this person has HIV/AIDS! I will say this again because it's very important; if you are sexually assaulted you can do ANYTHING, all the way up to ending their life if necessary to prevent the violation.

If we are to discuss the subject of lethal force, we must also address the carry and use of weapons. Carrying weapons is a huge responsibility. If you are going to carry them and potentially use them to protect yourself, get proper training…and maintain it! This not only ensures that you will be competent and safe with your tool(s); it demonstrates your responsibility later in court. It helps prove that you're not some crazy person with a deadly weapon on the loose in society.

ADVICE ON CARRYING WEAPONS:

IF YOU INTEND TO CARRY A WEAPON, THERE ARE A FEW THINGS YOU HAVE TO SERIOUSLY ASK YOURSELF FIRST:

- CAN YOU CARRY A WEAPON COMFORTABLY AND EASILY? IF YOU CAN'T, YOU WON'T.

- CAN YOU ACTUALLY KILL ANOTHER PERSON? IF YOU DON'T THINK YOU CAN, DON'T CARRY A WEAPON. IF YOU CARRY ONE AND CAN'T USE IT, IT WILL LIKELY BE USED ON YOU.

- ARE YOU PREPARED TODAY TO DEAL WITH THE AFTERMATH OF A LETHAL FORCE ENCOUNTER? THIS ONE'S TOUGH, BECAUSE IT TAKES TRUE INTROSPECTION. WHAT DO YOU STAND TO LOSE IF YOU KILL SOMEONE, EVEN IN SELF-DEFENSE? CAN YOU BE OKAY WITH THAT? ONLY YOU CAN ANSWER THIS.

THERE IS NO PLACE FOR MACHISMO OR "SHOW-BOATING" IN THE WORLD OF SELF-DEFENSE. IF YOU CARRY A WEAPON, NO ONE SHOULD KNOW. DON'T CARRY A GUN BECAUSE YOU WANT TO LOOK "COOL" OR TOUGH. IF SOMEONE SEES YOUR WEAPON AND GETS SCARED, YOU COULD HAVE A VERY BAD DAY. YOU MAY END UP WITH THOUSANDS OF DOLLARS IN FINES, OR WORSE YET, YOU COULD BE SHOT BY AN ARMED CITIZEN OR A POLICE OFFICER.

KNIVES –

IF YOU CARRY A KNIFE FOR SELF-DEFENSE, BE SURE IT HAS THESE KEY FEATURES:

- A QUALITY LOCKING MECHANISM

- EASY, ONE-HANDED OPENING

- GOOD GRIP TO AVOID SLIPPING

- AT LEAST A PARTIALLY SERRATED EDGE

A KNIFE CARRIED FOR SELF-DEFENSE SHOULD NOT HAVE A COMBAT ORIENTED NAME LIKE, "NAVY SEAL KILLER III". THE NAME SHOULD SOUND BENIGN AND "TOOL-LIKE" IN COURT.

A KNIFE SHOULD NOT BE CARRIED IN THE CONVENTIONAL "FRONT POCKET CLIP" LOCATION. THIS PLACEMENT IS NOT ONLY OBVIOUS, IT ALLOWS AN ATTACKER EASY ACCESS YOUR WEAPON. I RECOMMEND THE REAR BELT LINE OR BACK POCKET AS GOOD ALTERNATIVES.

GUNS –

GET A CONCEALED HANDGUN LICENSE. THEY ARE NOT THAT EXPENSIVE, AND PROVIDED YOU HAVE A CLEAN BACKGROUND, THEY ARE PRETTY EASY TO GET.

TAKE LIVE TRAINING COURSES THAT INCLUDE "POINT SHOOTING" SKILLS. RANGE PRACTICE IS FINE, BUT THAT WON'T PREPARE YOU FOR A COMBATIVE SHOOTING.

HAVE SOLID HAND-TO-HAND SKILLS TO SUPPORT YOUR FIREARM. IF YOU CANNOT FEND SOMEONE OFF EMPTY HANDED, IT'S HIGHLY UNLIKELY YOU WILL BE ABLE TO ACCESS YOUR WEAPON UNDER DURESS. MOST SHOOTINGS HAPPEN AT A RANGE OF LESS THAN 5 METERS. MOST OF THOSE INVOLVE SOME FORM OF HAND-TO-HAND STRUGGLE AS WELL. KEEP THIS IN MIND IF YOU DECIDE THAT CARRYING A GUN IS THE BEST WAY FOR YOU TO DEFEND YOURSELF.

PRACTICE DRAWING YOUR WEAPON. BE SURE TO FOLLOW STRICT SAFETY PRECAUTIONS. NEVER PRACTICE WITH A LOADED GUN! I RECOMMEND BUYING A PLASTIC REPLICA OF YOUR FIREARM. LOOK UP "BLUE GUNS" ON ANY WEB SEARCH AND YOU'LL FIND THEM.

CONCEALED MEANS CONCEALED. DON'T EVER SHOW OFF YOUR GUN! NO ONE SHOULD EVER KNOW THAT YOU CARRY.

DON'T DRAW YOUR GUN UNLESS YOU MEAN TO USE IT. A GUN IS NOT FOR INTIMIDATING PEOPLE OR LOOKING COOL…IT'S TO NEUTRALIZE A DEADLY THREAT, PERIOD.

When evaluating the appropriateness of your use of force during the court proceeding, the judge and jury will consider the "Totality of the Circumstances". This means that the court will consider factors like any disparity of size or numbers, the relative age and health of the people involved, the presence of a weapon, the criminal history of the parties involved, known threats based on restraining orders, etc. There is no simple black and white answer or guide to behavior. Again, your best bet is to follow the rule, "Do only what you must to stop the threat...and then stop immediately." The use of force is only authorized to get away from a dangerous situation, not to establish dominance.

Once we have a use-of-force policy in place, we need to develop an understanding of adrenal stress dynamics. If you are going to get physical, there are some physiological things that will occur...and they are out of your control. In moments of high stress, the autonomic nervous system (ANS) has several instinctive defensive measures it takes without conscious thought or intervention.

So, first of all, what's the ANS? The ANS is basically a regulatory brain function. The ANS is controlled by the hypothalamus and medulla oblongata at the base of the brain. The ANS regulates involuntary muscles, cardiac function, and the function of several glands. The ANS can be subdivided into two divisions, the sympathetic and the parasympathetic. The parasympathetic nervous system (PNS) controls higher reasoning, logic, and fine motor control. Fine motor control refers to the ability make specific movements with accuracy and precision (many martial arts techniques fall into this category). The sympathetic nervous system (SNS) controls involuntary startle-flinch responses, gross motor skills, and raw survival instincts. If properly enhanced, the instincts contained in these behaviors can be used to mount a formidable defense.

Basic Flinches

The human body comes hard-wired with natural defensive responses, and they are actually quite effective. In fact, forensics has shown us that startle-flinch responses occur within 1/10 of a second! It is unnecessary, and even counterproductive to try to re-train the body to make un-natural, non-instinctive "blocking" motions. The human body has three primary upper body defensive flinches that we can simply enhance:

1) We push danger away by extending our arms. Imagine someone suddenly falling forward into you. Your hands would instinctively reach out to push the weight away from you. The most effective modification to this flinch-response is known as the "Spear" tactic. Canadian tactical trainer Tony Blauer is responsible for developing this concept. To perform a Spear as effectively as possible, keep your arms at more than a 90 degree angle at the elbows, splay your fingers open in order to engage the incredibly strong extensor muscles, keep your hands in front of your eye-line, raise your shoulders high enough to protect your chin, and lunge forward slamming your forearms into the aggressor's incoming neck, shoulder, and attacking arm. The more of your body weight you drive into them, the more effective the defense. As they fall backwards or stutter-step to recover, you have the opportunity to disengage or initiate a defensive countermeasure.

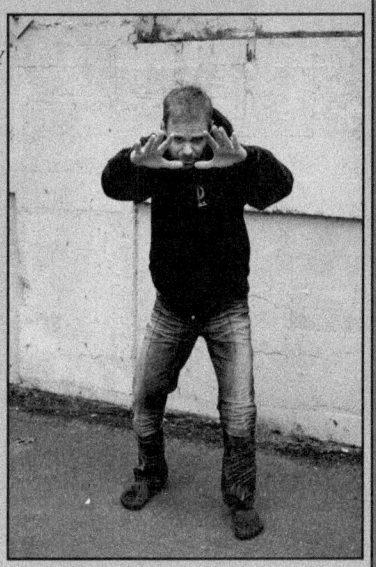

2) We parry incoming impacts away with slapping motions of our hands. The best way to represent this is to think of a bug flying at your eyeball. You don't Karate chop or cross-block at it…you swat it away without thought.

A slight impact to an incoming limb can greatly affect its trajectory, and thus its ability to hit the intended target. Boxers use this skill to deflect punches. Many systems of martial arts use "inside" and "outside" blocks that function much in the same way. No enhancement is necessary for this skill. The key is simply to not over-commit with these types of movements. Wildly waving your arms about in the air to deflect potentially incoming strikes leaves you vulnerable to counter strikes and combination punches.

3) We cover our heads with our arms and turn away from danger. This happens when something is likely to collide with the head. To enhance this instinct, simply grab the back of your head with both hands and wrap your arms around the sides of your skull, bringing your elbows to the front of your face. This forms a defensive shell that will shield the fragile bones of your face, your neck and throat, the thin temporal region of the skull, as well as the occipital region of the skull…which controls vision and consciousness. While you cannot remain in this position and indefinitely absorb damage, it does provide enough protection to weather a short barrage. This may be long enough to body check them, or counter with a defensive measure of your own.

Once we perceive a threat of significance, our body undergoes a series of chemical changes to prepare us for battle. Here is an abbreviated explanation: the adrenal gland (adrenal medulla) releases epinephrine (adrenaline) and nor-epinepherine (nor-adrenaline) into the bloodstream. Epinepherine and nor-epinepherine are hormones that prolong and intensify sympathetic nerve fiber stimulation. Sympathetic nerve fibers are the "hard wiring", if you will, to the SNS. Essentially, as the SNS is called upon for defense, the PNS temporarily relinquishes general system control to the SNS. Under the psychological stress of combat, we can only access information that is instinctual. We remain in this primal state until chemical homeostasis is restored and the PNS can resume its normal functions. People are often "jacked up" after a confrontation or a traumatic event for some time. We also begin to notice several other side effects of the adrenal rush:

Increased heart rate/blood pressure

The heart beats faster to move oxygen quickly to all of the parts of the body that are about to need more energy. During adrenal stress, heart rate can exceed 220 BPM. At 115 BPM fine motor skill begins to deteriorate, at 145 complex motor skill deteriorates, at 175 BPM cognitive processing deteriorates, and at 220 BPM you are in a state of hyper vigilance…possibly demonstrating irrational behavior.

Increased respiratory rate

As with increased heart rate, your respirations will increase as well. The idea is the same. The body is trying to store and process as much oxygen as possible for the upcoming fight or flight.

Dry mouth

When under adrenal stress, the body shuts down non-essential systems and functions, such as digestion. The salivary glands cease to produce saliva, as eating is no longer a priority of any kind. This can make talking difficult and a bit frustrating.

Sweaty palms

As blood moves away from the core and into the limbs to fight or run, the increased pressure and blood flow warms the limbs. Sweating is a natural method of cooling. Unfortunately, sweaty palms often mean a crappy grip.

Nausea

Again, as the body doesn't want to devote energy resources to nutrition when under imminent physical threat, the stomach stops processing food. The resulting shut down can register as nausea. If the stomach is full, it may evacuate itself to conserve energy and "lighten the load" for an escape. People often vomit under severe stress.

Change in voice

As the chemical cocktail rushes through the body, muscles constrict. This includes muscles in the neck and throat. When adrenalized, the vocal cords can quiver or spasm under the strain. If this happens as you try to speak, your voice will sound squeaky.

Tachi psyche

This is a fancy name used to describe the effect of time seemingly slowing down. People often report that under adrenal stress they feel like time slows down. They describe the effect as similar to a slow-motion video camera. In reality, our brain is just devoting more attention to details it would normally ignore or subconsciously process.

Tunnel vision

When we focus on something, we tend to block out other distractions. Consider watching TV. If you are into your show, you notice little else. When under adrenal stress, our autonomic nervous system tells us to pay attention to the problem at hand. This is our brain's way of devoting its full resources to solving the problem.

If you are unprepared and unaccustomed to these sensations, the adrenal rush can be overwhelming. The adrenal rush happens to everyone; even the most highly trained professional soldiers in the world. The reason they perform well under adrenal stress is their extensive scenario-based training. Scenario training can condition the body and mind to the extreme nature of violence induced stress. After the proper training from a qualified instructor, you will notice that adrenal stress becomes less "scary" and more recognizable as a defensive mechanism. Once you readily recognize that the adrenal rush makes you faster, stronger, and more resilient…you almost become super-human! When you are adrenalized, your body is automatically doing what is most efficient to ensure your survival. Trust and enhance your body's instincts; don't fear them.

Realities of Fighting

In the movies, fights are glorious! The hero battles bad guy after bad guy, handily defeating them all without sustaining much, if any damage. He easily takes multiple blows from his assailants, shucking them off without care. Hundreds of punches and kicks are thrown. Each technique is perfectly timed and delivered, making for a clean, snappy looking presentation. Real fights are nothing like this. Real fights are sloppy, chaotic, and unpredictable. Techniques rarely look "pretty" or land perfectly. Even if you practice martial skills regularly, in a real situation, they are going to lose some of their integrity just based on raw chemistry. Also, when engaged in violent activities…injuries are common. Even if you prevail, you are likely to sustain damage.

You cannot afford to take gratuitous damage. Fortunately, violent encounters tend to last an average of 10-30 seconds. Fights that go beyond that are wars! In all of my years of martial training and public safety, I can count on one hand the number of times a fight lasted longer than 30 seconds…and none passed the two minute mark.

When it hits the fan, keep things simple. Simple is better. There is concept known as "Hick's Law" that basically states that the less choices you have, the faster you can make a decision. Therefore it's better to be good at a small number of fighting techniques, than to have a huge inventory of moves. Because you won't be able to think straight and your body won't be capable of fine motor function, I recommend you limit your fighting moves to approximately five gross-motor based techniques.

This doesn't mean you don't have to train, in fact, quite the contrary. Train your body to respond under pressure. Adrenal stress conditioning via scenario-based drills is a great way to get your body and mind ready for conflict. Actually having to act out situations you may face in real life is the best way to gain experience, without risking your life.

There is a saying in the self defense industry, "You don't rise to the level of your expectations, you rise to the level of your training". Better have some, and it had better be good.

Have clear victory conditions. Victory doesn't mean standing over the broken corpse of your defeated adversary with your arms raised in triumph; it means you get to continue to survive. You may be responsible for more than just your safety. In that case, the survival and escape of those in your care is the primary victory condition. Don't get tunnel vision on "beating" an aggressor or buy into the Hollywood "Superhero" image.

REALITY CHECK: A MAN, WE'LL CALL HIM JIM, TOOK HIS WIFE AND TWO KIDS OUT TO A BASEBALL GAME. THEY SAT OFF THE THIRD BASE LINE A FEW ROWS BACK IN THE BLEACHERS. AT ONE POINT DURING THE GAME, AN UPSET BATTER CARELESSLY THREW HIS BAT BACK INTO THE STANDS. THE HEAVY BASEBALL BAT STRUCK JIM'S WIFE IN THE FACE, INSTANTLY SHATTERING HER JAW, BREAKING HER NOSE, AND SPLITTING HER FACE WIDE OPEN. SHE SUBSEQUENTLY FELL FORWARD INTO THE SPACE BETWEEN THE SEATS. JIM IMMEDIATELY DOVE ACROSS THE ROWS OF FANS, JUMPED ONTO THE FIELD, TACKLED THE BATTER, AND BEGAN BEATING THE HELL OUT OF HIM. THE TEAMS RUSHED IN AND BROKE UP THE FIGHT, BUT NOT BEFORE THE CROWD HAD STAMPEDED FORWARD TO GET A BETTER VIEW OF THE BRAWL. IN THE PROCESS, JIM'S WIFE SUFFERED FURTHER INJURIES IN THE FORM OF A BROKEN ARM AND RIB FROM BEING STEPPED ON BY THE UNRULY CROWD. THEIR TWO CHILDREN WERE HYSTERICALLY CRYING AND TRYING TO GET TO THEIR WOUNDED MOTHER.

THE BATTER WAS WEARING A JERSEY WITH HIS NAME AND NUMBER ON IT. HE WAS GOING NOWHERE. JIM SHOULD HAVE IMMEDIATELY ATTENDED TO HIS WIFE AND MOVED HIS FAMILY TO A SAFE PLACE WHERE HIS WIFE COULD RECEIVE MEDICAL ATTENTION. JIM WAS TOO EMOTIONALLY INVOLVED, GOT TUNNEL VISION, AND PRIORITIZED INCORRECTLY. FORTUNATELY, NO ONE DIED.

In reality, people are rarely alone. Dealing with more than one aggressor at a time is quite common. When you are considering your victory conditions, consider the disparity of numbers. If the numbers aren't on your side, the odds aren't either. If you must engage more than one person at a time, stack them in front of each other to nullify their numbers. Stacking is a term that describes keeping multiple aggressors in each other's way. Move yourself in such a way that the nearest attacker becomes a human shield against the others. Be mindful not to allow any of the aggressors to flank you. Agile footwork is the key here. If you are overwhelmed, and cannot stack them fast enough, sprint forward and body slam your way through the crowd at the point you perceive to be weakest. Try and gain distance to escape. If you cannot get away in time, go back to stacking them.

If you are forced to physically defend yourself, witnesses may not see the whole event. It's possible that witnesses will come out and take notice only after you have acquired the upper hand. If they come out, and see you on top of a bloody bad guy…they may assume YOU are the bad guy. If others approach, tell them to call 911 if they want to help. This will signify that you are the good guy (as bad guys don't want anyone calling the cops) and it gives them something to do other than interfering.

Tactical Disengagement

Tactical disengagement is our first choice of action. In some cases, we can skip from the threat recognition phase right to this step. If there is a threat we can avoid, hopefully we intelligently head for safety rather than managing the threat. Remember, a problem avoided is better than a problem solved. We only fight to provide an opportunity to tactically disengage. There are several key steps to an effective tactical disengagement.

Identify a safe zone

As mentioned before, a safe zone is any place with lots of people. Public facilities, professional establishments, and heavily populated locations provide lots of potential assistance. This, of course, doesn't guarantee that anyone will assist you, but the bad guy may not want to risk the attention.

Determine an escape route

Your active scan should always be looking for escape routes and exits. You can't run to safety if there's no way to get there.

Create distance

Once the physical conflict comes to a conclusion, there will have to be a moment of separation. This moment can be very dangerous. How you disengage is of significant importance. The following are some suggestions on effective tactical disengagement.

NEVER turn your back to a known threat. To do so exposes one of your most vulnerable areas. You may think you incapacitated them or that they were done fighting, but things aren't always what they appear. If you have to get up off of the ground, get up facing them. Don't roll over to your knees and crawl away or try to stand up facing away from them. If you turn your back, you may not see the attack that takes you out.

Along the same lines, if you are on top of someone on the ground, and you decide to dismount, do so carefully. Don't stand up with your legs on either side of their torso. The resulting "A" frame shape makes a convenient target for a swift kick to the groin. It's wiser to shift one knee onto their hip/belly area, push their face away with your hands, and stand up beside them.

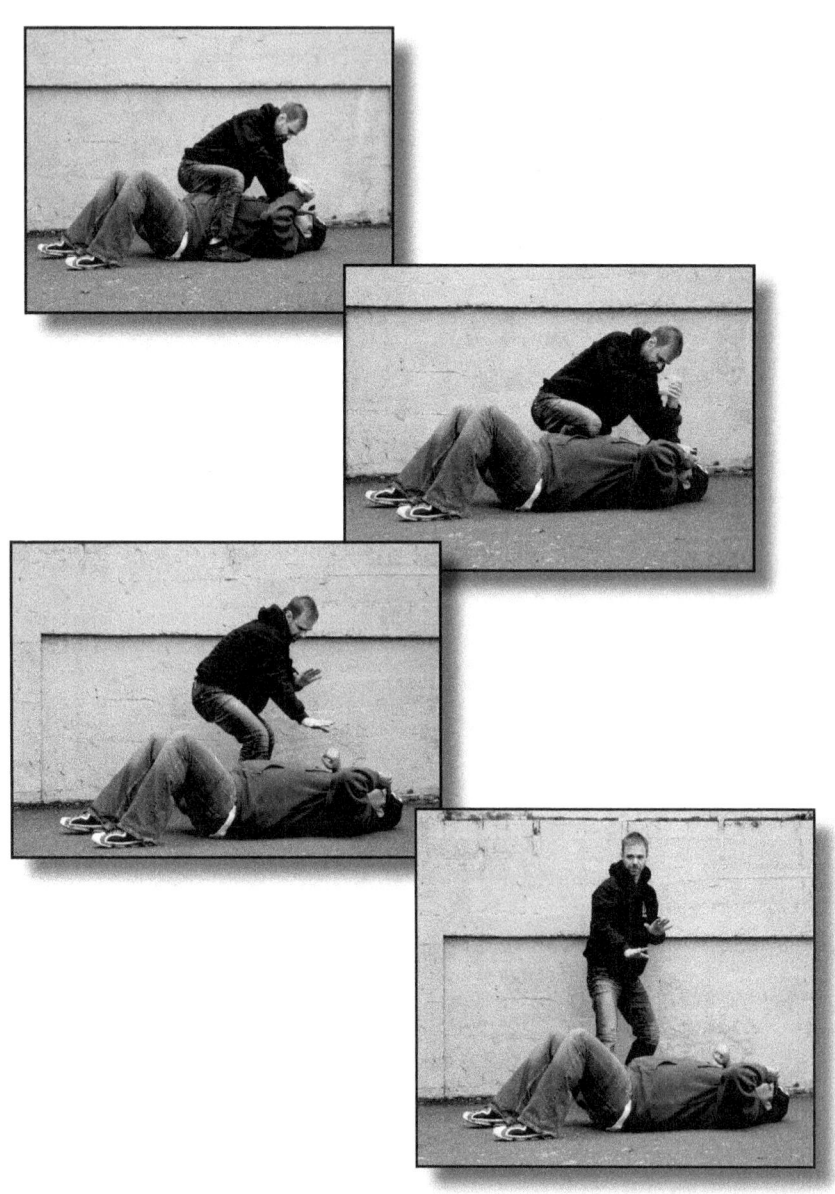

If you are on your back, and they are moving away from you, kangaroo kick them off of you as you initiate your recovery. The Kangaroo kick off is just an explosive leg press. Simply press the soles of your feet on the subject and shove off as hard as you can.

If you are standing facing an attacker, a firm push to the head or body may help create space between the two of you. I suggest the head as the primary target because where the head goes, the body follows. If you shove their head away from you, their whole body is going to move away and their balance will be compromised. Pushing the body requires more force to produce similar results.

Once they are separated from you, initiate a 360-degree scan and move to safety. Locate a safe zone. A safe zone is any place that has lots of people present and hopefully some cover. Establishments with security agents make great choices. Be aware of your surroundings. Don't leave a bad situation only to run right into a worse one. Never run away from danger…run to safety. Get to a safe zone and call 911.

In the cases of random acts of violence such as drive-by or mass shootings, the idea is to "hit-the-deck" (or get down on the ground to become less of a target) and hustle your behind to some cover. From there, tactically disengage from the threat. Even if you are an armed citizen, the goal of a gunfight is always to get away from the other person who is shooting at you. At the first opportunity to safely disengage, do it.

Aid and Evacuation

If you or someone you are with is injured during the course of an attack, try and get to a safe location before rendering significant medical aid. Remaining in the danger zone may get you both hurt worse. If you need to move them yourself, there are a few rescue extraction techniques you may find useful.

Assisted walk

To assist another in walking, drape one of their arms around the back of your neck. Use one of your arms to support them under the armpit or around the waist. Be sure to keep your shoulders low enough that they can lean their weight onto you.

Cradle carry

The cradle carry is designed for lifting those much lighter than you. Petite women and children are easily carried in this manner. To perform a cradle carry, bend at the knees while keeping your back straight, scoop one arm under both of the victim's knees and the other arm under their shoulder area, and stand up using the legs to lift the weight.

Fireman's carry

This technique uses the structure of your skeleton to support the weight of another. If they are too heavy to lift using a cradle carry, the fireman's carry is a good alternative. To perform a fireman's carry, you must place them into a seated position, underhook their armpits with your arms, lift them into an upright position, pass yourself under one of their arms as you turn to face them, duck your shoulder beneath their center mass while draping their arms and torso over your shoulder, and stand using your legs to lift them up. This technique takes a little practice to get the feel for the balancing points, but it is the most economical way to carry significant weight.

Body drag

If you simply can't lift the person you are trying to extract, the body drag is your final option. To perform a body drag, lift their upper body into an upright position. Crouch down behind them keeping your back straight. Encircle your arms under their armpits to the front of their body. Lift them slightly off the ground as you literally drag them backwards to safety.

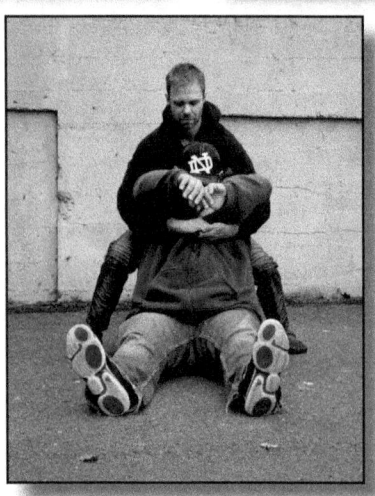

Medical Aid

I highly recommend that you maintain regular first aid training. Even from a non-combative perspective, having emergency medical competence can be a valuable life skill. Because the focus of this work is to address violence, I feel inclined to include a few emergency medical tips. This section in no way takes the place of an actual first aid class, but it will address some key areas of emergency aid.

A,B,C's

This acronym stands for airway, breathing, and circulation. These are key elements to assess in the instant observation process. When assessing the airway, we are checking for adequate ventilation and free passage of air into the lungs. If they are conscious and talking, we know we're good there. If they are unconscious, we need to check for breathing by looking and feeling for a rise and fall of the chest walls and listening for the passing of air. If they are not breathing properly, then we need to manually open their airway for them. In general the suggested method for this is called the head-tilt, chin-lift technique. To perform a head-tilt, chin-lift technique, gently place one hand on the patient's forehead and the fingers of the other hand under the patient's chin. Carefully lift the chin upward while tilting the forehead back to open the airway.

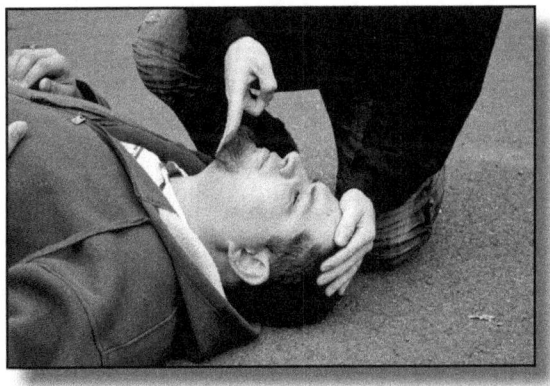

With patients that have suffered possible head, neck, or spinal wounds, the preferred method of opening an airway is using the jaw-thrust maneuver. To perform a jaw-thrust, place one hand on either side of the victim's head, support your body weight on your elbows, secure the angle of the jaw with your fingers and press their lower jaw open with your thumbs.

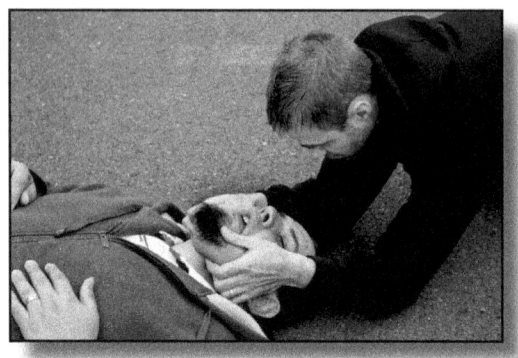

Circulation refers to the blood moving through the body. The main places to check the speed and intensity of the pump as well as the consistency of the pressurized system are at the radial and carotid pulse points. The radial pulse can be located on the inside of the wrist on the thumb side, below the fleshy part of the hand. There is a divot against the radial bone where the radial arteries travel across the boney surface. By gently pressing your index and middle fingers down on this point, you will feel the pulse as the arteries expand and contract with each heartbeat. Be mindful not to use a thumb to check for a pulse. The thumb registers its own arterial pulse. When checking the pulse of an unresponsive person, it's easiest to simply check the carotid pulse point. The carotid point can be found in the groove between the windpipe and the muscle of the neck. Again, press your two fingers into the artery and feel for the arterial pulse.

If the blood is obviously moving out of the body in large quantities…that's a problem. The body only holds between 3.5 and 5 liters of blood. When the body loses a small percentage of that, it begins to go into shock. Shock is a condition where blood doesn't effectively perfuse through the body.

Treatment for bleeding wounds follows this formula:

Apply direct pressure

Place a clean, sterile dressing directly on the wound and press firmly. If you have a first aid kit handy, gauze can be used to make a quick pressure bandage. In the unfortunate event that there are no medical supplies available, relatively clean clothing can make an acceptable supplement in a pinch. No cloth available? Use your hand.

Elevate the wound above the heart

Keeping the dressing in place, elevate the wound. If the wound is higher than the pump, you will minimize gravity's effect and reduce the "spill factor". If blood is going to leave the wound, it's going to have to be pumped out at the most difficult gravitational point.

Pressure point control

There are places where key arterial branches pass directly over bone. By applying pressure with the fingers to these places, we effectively "kink the hose". We actually pinch the arteries shut to reduce blood flow to the injured area until it can be closed. The idea is to apply pressure to the point directly above the wound. The main pressure points are:

Axillary (in the armpit)

Brachial (mid-shaft on the inside of the upper arm)

Radial (at the wrist pulse point)

Femoral (inside of inner thigh)

Apply a tourniquet

A tourniquet is the tying off of a limb just above the wounded area. By applying a tourniquet you are essentially writing off the damaged limb. Limbs that are placed in a tourniquet for any length of time are usually surgically amputated later. If someone has sustained a bullet wound or some other serious trauma to a limb, a belt or tied off cloth can serve as a makeshift tourniquet.

Managing Other Common Wounds:

Punctures

If an item is impaled into any part of the anatomy, DO NOT remove it! The very thing that punctured the body may very well be plugging an artery. If you remove the impaled object, the hole will become unobstructed and the blood will rush out. This could prove fatal.

Bullet wounds

As guns are tools of violence, it stands to reason that sometimes people get shot during violent encounters. Unfortunately, bullet wounds are complex injuries that require surgical intervention. Even the emergency medical practice of preparing an occlusive dressing is a somewhat complicated process, and it's unlikely you will be prepared or equipped to do this. As this injury is beyond your ability to treat in the field, your best bet is to get qualified medical aid there as fast as possible.

Managing a head wound

Head wounds are common during violent encounters. Blows to the head are bad and result in a variety of injuries, but the head falling or being slammed against hard surfaces is generally worse. It's actually quite common for people to suffer skull fractures, fall into comas and even die from falling unconscious and hitting the head on the ground. If you have to manage a head wound, check to see if they are conscious and assess their A,B,C's. Look to see if any pink fluid is leaking from their ears, nose, or mouth. Cerebral spinal fluid (CSF) is a pinkish color. It's the fluid that surrounds the brain and spinal cord. If this sign is present, it signifies a severe brain trauma. Apply pressure to any areas that are bleeding heavily. Unfortunately, most head wounds bleed a lot. The head, neck, and face are very vascular. Once you have addressed any major bleeding, secure the cervical vertebrae of their neck to prevent them from moving their head around. You don't want to allow damage to occur to the spinal cord or the already traumatized brain. You will also likely have to treat for shock.

Emergency treatment for shock

Elevate the patient's legs 8 to 12 inches if their injuries permit. Maintain their body temperature, as people with poor perfusion lose this ability. Keep them warm and covered, unless the environmental temperature exceeds 95 degrees Fahrenheit. Be sure to keep an eye on their airway. They are already in a fragile state. Respiratory failure at this point may very well result in death. Depending on their wounds, moving someone in a severe state of shock can kill them.

Violent encounters often result in injuries. Even if you prevail, it is highly probable that you will sustain some sort of wound. This becomes even more likely if you are responsible for defending others. In such times, it may become necessary to use your body as a shield that absorbs damage meant for another. Being capable of surviving until you can access help is as important as any combative skill. If, as mentioned above, you are responsible for protecting others, you would not be very effective if you couldn't manage basic wounds. To ensure complete personal safety, it is imperative that you know basic first aid.

First aid classes are taught at community colleges, fire stations, and Red Cross facilities throughout the nation. They are generally inexpensive and well worthwhile. You don't need to become a professional medic; you just need to understand the basics of emergency medicine. Most first responder classes are only a few hours long. To be an effective first responder, it helps to have a decent first aid kit. It is not difficult to put together a custom first aid kit but, there are many quality kits that you can buy pre-assembled at the local drug store. I recommend choosing kits with the largest bandages you can carry around. These types of first aid kits are easily stored in cars, bags, briefcases, etc. Even if you never need them for a serious emergency, you'll be surprised how often someone needs a band-aid.

Post-Conflict Police Interaction

After a conflict is over or perhaps before it's over, the police are likely to arrive. They usually don't have all of the answers and they don't know who all of the players are. When they show up, cooperate. Do what they tell you to do. Keep your hands visible and make it very clear that you intend no hostilities. They may very well think you are the bad guy. Expect to be treated like a criminal until they sort things out.

Be respectful, but be mindful of what you say. You will be in an adrenalized state. The police are going to want answers, and you will also be held accountable in court for anything you say…even under these conditions. Truthfully, it can be difficult to recall details right after a traumatic event. Let them know that you wish to cooperate, but that you are a little shaken up. If you need a break from the questioning, ask for an EMT to evaluate you. When you do speak to the officers, articulate the steps you took to avoid the problem and the operational security model that you routinely follow. Explain why you couldn't just leave, and why you had no other choice but to act. Don't go into a bunch of detail; just give them the highlights. If they want more information, don't be afraid to ask for an attorney.

Conclusion

Regardless of the classification, violence is a part of life. Whether we like it or not, we are likely to confront it on some level. As such, it only makes sense to prepare. Following a standard operational security model is a big part of staying safe. So is training. Be sure that your training regimen fits your needs and prepares you for reality.

Scenario training and verbal de-escalation tactics should account for a significant amount of your training time. Physical skills should focus on enhancing natural instincts, managing impacts and armed assaults, and escapes from positions of disadvantage. Keep in mind, self defense is not about "beating people up"…it's about disengaging from a bad situation safely. If you find that you're spending most of your time punching, kicking, pursuing submission holds, or becoming proficient with a weapon…I suggest you may want to re-evaluate your training based on real priorities. We all have a tendency to do what we're good at. The idea is to get better at what you're not good at.

Sources

I'm a big believer in credit where credit is due. When it comes to the information presented in this manual, lots of folks deserve credit. Over the years, I have assembled what I consider to be the best, most useful personal safety information from the top experts in the industry. Notice I said assembled. I don't claim to be the founder of a "new" combat system or a supreme great grandmaster of a martial lineage. I haven't created anything new. In fact, there is really nothing new under the sun. My contribution has been the gathering and organization of the purest most reliable information. The only thing that I claim to have developed is the seven step operational security model (OSM) that I use to present the information I share.

The people who deserve recognition as sources used in this work are many:

Sgt. Rory Miller, bestselling author, Veteran Correctional/Tactical Officer

- Meditations on Violence, A Comparison of Martial Arts Training & Real World Violence – YMMA Publication Center, 2008

- Facing Violence, Preparing for the Unexpected – YMMA Publication Center, 2011

Rory Miller's work greatly contributed to both the threat recognition and legal portions of this work.

George J. Thompson, Ph.D., bestselling author, World Renowned Conflict Management Trainer

- Verbal Judo, The Gentle Art of Persuasion– William Morrow, 2004

A significant amount of Dr. Thompson's work was referenced in the Diffusion and De-escalation section.

Richard Dimitri, author, World Renowned Personal Defense Trainer, Founder of Senshido

- In Total Defense of the Self – Senshido, 1994

Rich's information shows up in both the verbal de-escalation and defensive countermeasures sections. Rich is responsible for developing the most effective defensive countermeasure I have ever been exposed to, the "Shredder".

Tom Patire, noted author, Elite Bodyguard Trainer

- Tom Patire's Personal Protection Handbook – Three Rivers Press, 2003

Many of the safety and awareness tips are based on suggestions made by Mr. Patire.

Peyton Quinn, noted author, Rocky Mountain's Combat Applications Training Center (RMCAT) Trainer

- Bouncer's Guide to Bar Room Brawling, Dealing with the Sucker Puncher, Streetfighter, and Ambusher – Bouler, CO; Paladin Press, 1990
- Real Fighting, Adrenaline Stress Conditioning Through Scenario -Based Training – Boulder, CO; Paladin Press, 1996

Peyton Quinn is a pioneer in the area of combat oriented adrenal stress training. His work paved the way for much of the scenario-based training we see today. His work is referenced several times in the defensive countermeasures section.

Bruce K. Siddle, noted author, Adrenal Stress Trainer/Expert

- <u>Sharpening the Warrior's Edge, the Psychology & Science of training</u> – PPCT Research, 1995

Mr. Siddle continues with Peyton Quinn's work. His information was referenced in the same area.

Special Agent Robert Hazelwood, FBI Behavioral Science Instruction/Research Unit, Quantico, VA

- The Criminal Behavior of the Serial Rapist – Crime & Clues, 1998

A good portion of the data and information on verbal communication with rapists is based on Special Agent Hazelwood's work.

Major Avi Nardia, author, Military Tactical Expert, Kapap Chief Instructor

- <u>Kapap Combat Concepts, Martial Arts of the Israeli Special Forces</u> – Black Belt Communications, 2008

Major Nardia is responsible for coining the term "relative positional control". The concept of relative positional control is a key element in setting a personal perimeter as well engaging defensive countermeasures and tactically disengaging.

Tony Blauer, Tactical Trainer, Founder of the SPEAR system, and head honcho of Blauer Tactical Systems (BTS)

Tony Blauer is responsible for developing the startle-flinch enhancing defensive tactic known as the SPEAR (spontaneous protection enabling accelerated response)

California Police Officer Standards and Training (POST)

- <u>Criminal Law & Evidence Sourcebook, Peace officer's edition</u> – San Clemente, Ca., Law Tech, 1999

This text was referenced for the technical crime definitions and elements

U.S. Department of Justice (US DOJ)

Criminal statistics

Federal Bureau of Investigation (FBI)

Criminal statistics

Jesse Lawn is also available for lectures, seminars, and workshops. For more information, go to **www.jesselawn.com.**

www.ingramcontent.com/pod-product-compliance
Lightning Source LLC
LaVergne TN
LVHW051506070426
835507LV00022B/2952